D1613368

DEER STALKING IN BRITAIN

ALSO BY MICHAEL BRANDER

A Concise Guide to Game Shooting. The Sportsman's Press

Other books of sporting interest by the same author:
Sporting Pigeon Shooting
Gundogs: Their Care & Training
A Complete Guide to Horsemanship
Training The Pointer-Retriever
An Introduction to Trout Fishing
Groundgame
The Roughshooter's Sport
The Roughshooter's Dog
Hunting & Shooting
The Hunting Instinct
Portrait of a Hunt
etc.

DEER STALKING IN BRITAIN

MICHAEL BRANDER

Illustrated by
Christopher Wood

• THE •
SPORTSMAN'S
PRESS
LONDON

Published by The Sportsman's Press, 1986

© Michael Brander 1986
Illustrations © Christopher Wood 1986

All rights reserved. No part of this publication may be
reproduced, stored in a retrieval system, or transmitted
in any form or by any means, electronic, mechanical,
photocopying, recording or otherwise, without the prior
permission of the publishers.

British Library Cataloguing in Publication Data

Brander, Michael
Deer stalking in Britain.
1. Deer hunting – Great Britain
I. Title
799.2'77357   SK301

ISBN 0–948253–05–3

Photoset & printed in Great Britain by
Redwood Burn Limited, Trowbridge, Wiltshire

Contents

Illustrations

Preface and Acknowledgements

This is intended as an introduction to deer stalking both in woodland and on the open hill, dealing chiefly with roe and red deer, the two indigenous breeds, but also providing an introduction to fallow, sika, muntjac and Chinese water deer, should they be encountered. I am well aware that many books have already been written on the subject of deer and, indeed, most of them have been mentioned in the very wide-ranging critical bibliography. As will be seen from this, most aspects of deer and deer stalking or deer hunting, have been dealt with individually, but so far no book has covered all the species of deer likely to be encountered in the wild in this country, their background history, how they have been affected by hunting and stalking, and how the sports themselves have developed, as well as how to approach stalking today. This is intended as a fresh approach and in the way it is put together it is to be hoped that the beginner will find it useful, while even the experienced stalker may find something of interest, if only in the bibliography.

When I started stalking after the war it was with a .303 and open sights, a combination I already knew well enough from my schoolboy days onwards. In those early postwar years in the Border country of Scotland, roe deer, where very prevalent, were still frequently shot with shotguns and I shot a number cleanly enough in this way at close range then, although I am neither advocating this nor excusing it. Today I use a .243 or a .270 with the best telescopic sight I can find. Like most deer stalkers of any experience at all, I probably have my prejudices and may well have indicated some of them already, but as a fairly practiced author I have tried not to intrude my own views too obviously at any point. Whether I have succeeded or not it is up to the reader to decide.

My thanks and acknowledgements must go to many librarians throughout Scotland and the U.K., who have helped me by providing books for research through the Inter-library Loans Service, and in particular Mr Brian M. Gall, the Librarian, and Mr David Moody, and the very helpful Staff of the East Lothian District Library Service and also Mrs Gavan, the Librarian, and staff of the Haddington Library. My thanks must also go to my neighbour, and extremely experienced stalker, Dr Frank Holmes, author of that very interesting book *Following the Roe*, for taking on the tiresome task of reading the typescript and commenting on it, also to my wife Evelyn, Kenneth Grose and Phil Harris for the same boring chore. My thanks are also due to Christopher Wood for his very excellent illustrations. For any mistakes or omissions, however, I am entirely responsible.

Introduction

Since mankind first began to hunt with stone clubs and spears, deer, of one kind or another, have been amongst the principal creatures hunted. In almost every part of the world deer hunting has been the subject of art and literature since man first drew on cave walls, or scratched symbols on clay tablets. The literature on deer hunting in Britain starts with the work of William Twici, huntsman to Edward III, who wrote *Le Art de Venerie* in 1327, reprinted by Sir Henry Dryden with annotations in 1844 and by his daughter, Alice Dryden, in 1907. William Twici's book was followed by various others on hunting deer at intervals up to the nineteenth century, but it was not until 1839 that William Scrope wrote *Days of Deer Stalking*, the first book devoted solely to deer stalking.

Since then, over the past 145 years or so, although there have been a great number of books written on deer and deer stalking, as will be seen by glancing at the critical bibliography on pages 165/75, there have been scarcely any covering the whole gamut of the sport. There have been many excellent books written on various aspects of stalking, yet, strangely enough, only Frank Wallace and Lionel Edwards seem to have covered the whole spectrum of stalking and hunting the deer then found in the wild in both England and Scotland with their classic book written in the grand Edwardian style, *The Pursuit of Red, Fallow and Roe Deer in England and Scotland*, published in 1927 by Longmans and, of course, superbly illustrated by Lionel Edwards.

Since the 1920s, however, deer hunting and the sport of stalking have undergone a considerable revolution in this country. The two are still closely linked, in that, for instance, woodland stalking for red deer has much in common with the start of a deer hunt, so the first two chapters are an attempt to show how the various changes that have taken place in the history of this country have affected the countryside, the deer populations in it, and thus the sport connected with them. The remainder of the book covers the various species of deer now likely to be encountered in the wild, their habits and habitat, the methods of stalking them in woodland and on the open hill, the rifle and other equipment required, the shooting and where necessary the tracking of a wounded deer, as well as how to deal with the carcase, down to details of trophy measurements. Finally a glossary of terms used and a critical bibliography of many of the books written on deer over the past 150 years, should enable the complete beginner to know where to start and what is required before taking up stalking in one form or another.

That much of the material in this book is well-trodden ground to experienced stalkers cannot be avoided. There may well be points with which they disagree, but there may even be points they find helpful. It is intended simply as an overall introduction and general guide to the deer and the various forms of stalking available in England and Scotland.

By its very nature woodland deer stalking is a sport in which the individual very often has to be prepared to go out at unsocial hours and spend much of his time without any company, save possibly for a dog. On the other hand, on the hill in the highlands it may often be a question of relying largely on a professional stalker who knows the ground for guidance in all but shooting the deer. These are not everyone's ideas of amusement, or sport, but from this book the beginner should appreciate why hunting deer in all its forms is a sport which appeals to many people and from which a great deal of elemental satisfaction can be obtained, even if very few shots are fired each year.

It should be appreciated that the object of the whole exercise is to make those few shots fired serve their purpose efficiently. The professional stalker who fired only fifty shots and killed fifty deer in the course of the year might have performed his task with the maximum skill possible. As everyone involved in stalking deer knows, however, this is an ideal which simply cannot be achieved, because circumstances, not least time and the weather, would never permit it, but it still remains the ideal.

Possibly more than any other sport, stalking involves long hours spent in observation and anticipation, pitting one's own skills all the time against the acute senses of a wild creature, prior to becoming involved in the end in direct and often very physical action. That the shot is almost the least important part of the proceedings, although it is essential that it should be correctly aimed, is something which it may be difficult for those who have never stalked to understand. That it is so, is none the less the case.

In a rather more direct way than most sports the keynote of stalking is in large part the preservation and improvement of the species being stalked. Thus the hunter and the hunted have a direct link going back over the centuries as well as into the future. It may be hard for the bewildered anti-hunting lobby to understand, but as will be seen from the history of deer in Britain over the centuries, the only reason they have survived is that they have been hunted and were preserved for this purpose. When, for instance, the protection of the hunting laws was misguidedly withdrawn from them, roe deer were nearly exterminated. To stalk deer well it is necessary to understand them and to understand them is to wish to preserve them, which can only be done by efficient stalking and deer management. The two are and always have been directly related.

To
Ed Zern
The Orbiting Sportsman
(*v* Glossary and Bibliography)

1

Deer in Britain:
the Background to 1800
QUESTION AND ANSWER

Which deer are indigenous to Britain?

Only the roe deer (*Capreolus capreolus*) and the red deer (*Cervus elaphus scoticus*) are truly indigenous to Britain. Of the two, the roe is probably the older. It is notable that during the Pleistocene Age the roe appears to have been widely spread throughout Britain and the interesting feature is that heads of that period were, according to Millais, if anything slightly inferior to modern heads. This was certainly not the case with red deer heads of the same period which, along with the beasts themselves, seem to have been very much larger. They also appear to have been widely spread throughout many parts of Britain and remains are to be found in most Iron Age forts, particularly in areas of the Lowlands of Scotland where they are no longer to be found today.

When was the fallow deer introduced to this country?

The answer to this is largely conjecture. The fallow deer (*Dama dama*), although present in Prehistoric times, was apparently unable to survive the last Ice Age and was subsequently re-introduced to Britain, although exactly when and by whom is uncertain. Whether it was the Phoenicians, that great Mediterranean seafaring and merchant nation, or the Romans, who re-introduced the fallow deer to Britain, or whether, as with native cattle breeds, they were simply ferried across the channel from Gaul in the course of local trade, has still to be proved. There is no particular reason why the Phoenicians, the Romans and native tribes trading with the Gauls may not all at various times have introduced *Dama dama* into the country. Certainly, after two peaceful centuries of Roman rule prior to their departure in AD 407, it seems likely that at least a few small herds of *Dama dama* may have been established. Yet even supposing that several hundred fallow deer were introduced over this period and were encouraged to breed there is unfortunately no clear archaeological evidence of their presence in any great numbers. Then, with the departure of the Romans, they would have had to face numerous natural predators including wolves, as well as the incessant hunting inherent in unsettled times. It may also be fairly assumed that they were only to be found in limited numbers in certain areas, almost certainly chiefly in the south. Any that had not adapted to the wild were unlikely to be spared by the invading Saxons as they burned and pillaged the Roman villas prior to clearing settlements of their own.

What was the probable effect of the Saxon invasion on wildlife, particularly deer?

With the spread of a very parochial Christianity the Saxons tended to settle on the land, laying the foundations of the future parish areas through which the country was to be subdivided. The greater part of the countryside, however, remained still thickly wooded with numerous bears, wolves and wild boars still to be found. All deer would have been at risk and any *Dama dama* surviving would have had to contend with many predators in the wild. Nor were the Saxon hunting methods selective. They employed nets, pits, snares and deadfall traps, capable of catching anything from a wolf to a bear, or deer, but incapable of distinguishing between a rare species and one comparatively common. In particular they used a system of 'hayes', or semi-permanent fences half a mile or so in length, built on the stake and binder principle, sited in conjunction with others or else with some natural obstacle such as a cliff face, so that any animals driven into them from the surrounding area were funnelled past concealed groups of hunters waiting with nets, spears, bows and arrows and hunting dogs. These 'hayes' were highly prized and the rights to them appear to have passed down the families of the nobility. No doubt there were accepted laws and customs about their use, but all trace of them has now vanished along with the 'hayes' themselves. It is hardly likely that any beasts driven into them were spared because of their rarity, but rather that they were more highly prized on that account. On the credit side the Saxons deliberately set out to reduce the number of wolves by demanding a return of so many wolf skins as a form of taxation, thus introducing a primitive form of conservation.

When were the first laws on hunting introduced in Europe?

After the Saxons came successive invasions of Danes and Vikings so that the country remained in a highly unsettled state for several centuries, but on the Continent in the seventh century the Frankish king Dagobert formulated regulations regarding hunting and notable amongst these were severe penalties for killing any stalking deer, i.e. tame deer trained to be used as cover for a hunter stalking a herd with bow and arrow. It may be assumed that some of these valuable stalking deer were *Dama dama* and it may equally be assumed that some were imported by the Saxon and Danish nobility. It is thus likely that some fresh imports of *Dama dama* on a limited scale took place about this time so that if any breeding stock had survived it is probable they now had fresh blood brought into the country. It is also likely that such highly prized deer were preserved in specially enclosed parks specially set aside for them. Even so it is questionable if they were yet established to any real extent.

What were the Danish hunting methods?

It is clear from the Frankish hunting laws that one of the methods of hunting deer in the seventh century was by stalking a herd under cover of tame stalking deer, so that by approaching from downwind it was possible to get within bowshot. By using a tame hind it was also probably common to lure stags, or bucks, within bowshot during the rutting season. By the eighth century it may be safely assumed that both Danes and Saxons were copying such methods in Britain. It is certain they were also hunting with hounds, mostly on foot but sometimes mounted on horseback, as well as by the more primitive Saxon method of encircling large areas and driving their quarry to hunters waiting in concealed 'hayes' or similar hides. In addition, the use of nets and traps was still widespread, so that the wild deer had considerable hazards to face within range of any human habitation. On the other hand, since Saxon and Danish nobility were more or less permanently at war, the time they had to spare for hunting was necessarily limited. It was not until the reign of King Alfred the Great in AD 878 that Saxons and Danes achieved an uneasy peace and even then Viking raids around the coastline were a common occurrence.

When were the first hunting laws introduced in Britain?

It was not until the reign of Canute that an attempt was first made to formulate any laws on hunting in Britain. In 1016 the forerunner of all future Game Laws in Britain was enacted. It read in part:

'I will that each one shall be worthy of such venerie as he by hunting can take, either in the plain or in the woods within his own fee or dominion, but each man shall abstain from my venerie in every place where I will that my beasts shall have firm peace and quietness oppon the same to forfeit as much as any man may forfeit.'

Red deer on the hill

Even if the language is at first sight deceptively mild the meaning is plain enough. The penalty for hunting in the King's forests was death. Elsewhere the right to hunt went with the ownership, or overlordship, of the land. It is from this basis that the existing British principle evolved that game belongs to the landowner rather than to the state, as is almost universal everywhere else in the world. It is really only from this time onwards that it can be confidently assumed that any *Dama dama* introduced were likely to be left free to breed in peace. It seems reasonable to assume that there were still not many areas where they were as yet very firmly established in the wild. The odds were simply enormous against the survival of any species introduced into the wild during the six hundred years of turmoil since the departure of the Romans. It was only once a degree of peace was restored and some firm laws regarding the hunting of game were introduced that any species introduced into the wild could hope to survive, let alone thrive and multiply.

What effect did the Norman Conquest have on the deer population?

The ruling Normans, enthusiastic hunters of deer, ensured that the native deer were preserved for them to hunt and it may be safely assumed that they would import fresh stock from their own hunting grounds in Normandy and elsewhere in Europe if they felt there was any scarcity. From the Domesday Book it appears that by 1086 there were already thirty-one enclosed parks in various parts of southern England, some of which may have been in existence prior to the Conquest. Whether they were necessarily enclosing fallow deer as well as red, roe, wild boar and other game is open to question. It is, however, likely that the Normans did import and preserve fallow deer in parks and the final establishment of *Dama dama* as a part of the fauna of Britain is almost certainly due to them. It may be safely accepted therefore that fallow deer have been firmly established in Britain for nearly a thousand years.

How did the Normans organise hunting?

Almost all the hunting terms current in the English language today may be traced back to Norman French, e.g. *Il-est haut*, the cry when a beast was seen in full flight became by verbal transposition the modern cry of 'Tally-ho' and so on. They also took over and enforced Canute's Forest Laws with complete ruthlessness. Unfortunate Saxons were painfully executed for offences such as eating the remains of a boar they had found dead in the forest. No one save the King and his appointed nobles were allowed to hunt in any given area and in the King's forests only he might hunt. The returns of beasts killed, their skins and meat, were a useful addition to the Exchequer and as an economic and political weapon the Forest Laws were a major source of royal power until well into the Middle Ages and beyond. They were also, when strictly enforced, a continual source of complaint throughout the country from the nobility downwards. According to the Norman laws on hunting the beasts of venerie were 'The Hart, the Hind, the Hare, the Boar and the Wolf', while the beasts of the chase were 'the Buck, the Doe, the Fox, the Martin, and the Roe'. The red deer was thus highest on the list with the fallow a good deal lower and the roe last of all.

At this stage all the game was jealously preserved. The King himself had a number of royal forests. Indeed one of William I's first acts was to declare a large area of Hampshire a royal forest to be called the New Forest. Other forests were divided into chases, or areas delineated for hunting exclusively by certain nobility. Many of the nobility also had enclosed parks in which deer and other animals were preserved. It was a natural temptation for the owners of such parks to include specially constructed deer leaps in the walls, which allowed deer from the royal forest easy access into the park, but prevented their return. These were a frequent source of litigation and dispute over the centuries.

What were the Norman methods of hunting?

Along with the Norman-French hunting language the Norman methods of hunting completely superseded those of the Saxons and Danes and, like the Forest Laws, were to become the basis of modern hunting. There were two principal methods of hunting:

1 The favourite Norman way of hunting deer was *par force*. The huntsman had to find by means of the deer's tracks, or slots, and its droppings, or fewmets, where a suitable huntable beast was lying up, or harboured. Then, with deep-scenting hounds, the selected beast would be roused from its bed in the forest and hunted with both scenting hounds and greyhounds, or 'gaze hounds', the latter released to hunt only when the deer was in full view. Meanwhile the huntsmen and hunt followers, on horseback or on foot, followed as best they might through the forest or over open country. Finally when the deer was brought to bay it was despatched with spear or sword. The Normans regarded it as the height of skill, as indeed it was, for one man to execute each stage of the hunt, from finding where the hart was harboured, to hunting it and finally despatching it single-handed.

2 Using tame deer, or artificial deer made from cloth, individual archers might stalk deer feeding on the edge of the forest so as to get within range. No doubt archers would also station themselves, in the manner of modern marksmen in a high seat, in trees around places where deer were likely to pass on their way to feed. Still-hunting, or the stalking of deer in woodland by very slow and careful movement, was no doubt also practised, as well as driving game to waiting hunters, but with savage boars still liable to be encountered such hunting may at times have ended abruptly with the roles reversed and the hunter finding himself the hunted. All these latter forms of hunting, however, were secondary in the Norman view to hunting with hounds *par force*.

From the advent of the Normans onwards, throughout the Middle Ages, the countryside of Britain was very gradually becoming less wild. The process was remorseless and inevitable, even if it was to take four or five centuries before the last boars were killed and the forests considerably reduced by the demands for charcoal for smelting and timber for firewood and building.

How do we know about the changes in hunting methods?

The change is best mirrored perhaps in the early hunting literature. William Twici, huntsman to King Edward III, wrote his treatise on hunting, *Le Art de Venerie*, probably around 1327. He regarded the hare as the most difficult and satisfying beast to hunt, but he also wrote with enthusiasm on hunting deer of all kinds and went at some length into the correct use of the horn. Indeed, from his description, it would seem the forests must have resounded with the blowing of horns in those days for it was by this means the huntsmen kept in touch with each other during the hunt in dense forest, while following the baying of the hounds. It was nearly a hundred years later, around 1413, that Edward, Duke of York, Master of Game to Henry IV, wrote his book, *The Master of Game*, describing all forms of hunting. This was, however, little more than a translation of *La Livre de la Chasse*, written in the previous century by Gaston III, Count of Foix et Bearn in the Pyrenees, one of the greatest and most dedicated huntsmen of all time who wrote his notable book at some time around 1380.

What particular points may be noted from these books?

It is particularly noteworthy that both Twici and the Duke of York, copying Count Gaston Phoebus, referred to the roe deer as a good beast for hunting, since it appears that this was not the general consensus of opinion at the time. On the grounds that it 'drove away other deer' the roe was reduced from a beast 'of the forest' to a beast 'of warren' in 1338. This meant in effect that it was no longer so stringently protected by the Forest Laws. Naturally the result was that most countrymen considered it fair game and over the next few centuries it was widely persecuted and eventually seems to have been hunted or poached to extinction in many southern areas, while the fallow deer, on the contrary, proving ideal for keeping in parks and for hunting, like the red deer was more stringently protected and continued to spread throughout the country.

How were deer affected in Scotland during this period?

During the twelfth and thirteenth centuries the Scottish monarchy had developed on Norman feudal lines and there had been intermittent warfare with England. The Scottish nobility had hunted red and roe deer in the Lowlands and Highlands, both of which were still well afforested. Continual border warfare during the latter part of the thirteenth and most of the fourteenth centuries resulted in the disappearance of the forests and the red deer, although the roe probably survived in some areas. Some of the highland forests also began to disappear at the same time. The highland method of hunting, known as the Tainschel, or circle, however, remained similar to that of the Saxons with large tracts of ground encircled with beaters and driven towards well known deer passes, where hunters were waiting in ambush equipped with swords, spears, bows and arrows and deer hounds at the ready.

How did the Reformation affect sport and the countryside in England?

With the passing of the Middle Ages the old strict Forest Laws were widely ignored and in many places simply lapsed for want of enforcement, especially as many forests themselves were by this time much smaller than they had been owing to continual felling of trees for charcoal and building of both houses and ships. The dissolution of the monasteries also resulted in large areas of forest, hunting chases, deer parks and warrens changing hands. This was a time of change and flux in every sphere. It saw the beginning of the abandonment of the old open field feudal system of farming and the enclosing of erstwhile common land heralding the hedgerows and chequered landscape we still see around us today. It saw the introduction of the early matchlock and wheel-lock guns and the use of 'hayle shotte' forerunners of further changes. The new middle classes of the Tudors and of Elizabeth the First wished to emulate the old nobility, but they were also ready for change and willing to experiment.

What were the principal changes in hunting during the reigns of Henry VIII and Elizabeth I?

The reign of Henry VIII saw the passing of the old Norman form of *par force* hunting and a changeover to hunting mostly in the confines of a park. The satisfaction of this type of hunting depended not on the pace of the hunt, for the hounds were still mainly slow and clumsy as they had been in Norman times, but on the hound music. The Tudors matched their hounds for sound rather than size. They would set a buck loose in a park, sometimes having deliberately lamed it with a cross-bow and would then lay the variegated pack of hounds on the blood trail, but instead of following the hounds on horseback or on foot they would ride to a small knoll, or sit in a bower in the park, and listen to the voices of the individual hounds as each gave tongue, naming each in turn and following the progress of the hunt in this fashion. When the buck was finally brought to bay it might be despatched with a cross-bow. (A survival of this method of hunting is still practised with 'coon hounds in Kentucky.) They also coursed deer in the confines of the parks with greyhounds. John Selwyn, keeper of the royal deer park at Oteland, obviously a wiry nimble character, performed the celebrated feat of leaping onto the back of a hunted buck in 1587 and guided it with his hunting sword to the Queen's feet, where he killed it.

One reason for this increase of hunting inside enclosed parks may well have been the growing scarcity of huntable beasts. Since such enclosed parks might be of several thousand acres in extent this was not quite so limiting as might at first appear to be the case. Then again, as almost every squire kept his own pack of hounds which were prepared to hunt whatever they encountered, the game must have been much harried in some parts and no doubt the aristocracy thought it preferable to hunt without fear of possible interruption. It is notable that in 1591 Sir Thomas Cockaine in his fresh and original book, *A Short Treatise on Hunting*, was the first to expound on the advantages of foxhunting in the open as a worthwhile sport, something that had previously scarcely been considered and an indication of how scarce huntable beasts were becoming outside the confines of a park. He also noted that red deer were becoming scarce and that roe were good to hunt. There is little doubt that hunting methods were changing considerably in character over this period.

How did the accession of James I in 1603 affect deer hunting?

With that ill-fated Stuart insensitivity to people and events James I attempted to re-introduce *par force* hunting. It is an indication of how times had changed that he had to ask Henry IV of France to send him a huntsman who could teach his English huntsman how to set about it. He was apparently also forced to import a quantity of red deer from France at the same time, which indicates how greatly numbers had decreased, although it may merely have been that he felt new blood was required. He is certainly reputed to have imported dark fallow deer from Norway to Scotland and then, about 1620, to have had them brought down to Epping Forest, whence the notably dark strain of fallow is said to originate. He also set loose some wild boars in the royal forests as none remained.

No doubt he was accustomed to the old highland method of hunting, which still continued in the same time-honoured way with hundreds of deer being driven past waiting hunters. It is symptomatic of James's views on hunting and general Stuart insensitivity that when the Archbishop of Canterbury, shooting at deer with a cross-bow, accidentally shot and killed his headkeeper, Peter Hawkins, James merely advised him 'not to discomfort himself as such an accident might befall any man: his Queen in like sort killed him the best brache (hound) that he ever had.'

What were the principal developments affecting deer in the course of the seventeenth century?

The seventeenth century saw many dramatic happenings including, of course, the Civil Wars, amongst the greatest internal upheavals that have affected these islands. It is easy therefore to overlook minor details affecting side issues such as the movement of deer. It is interesting to note, however, that in 1633 Charles I sent for over thirty roe kids from Lord William Howard at Naworth in Cumberland to be released in Wimbledon Park. Unless he wanted fresh outside blood this would appear to indicate that by this time they were no longer easily to be found anywhere in the south. Apparently by 1639 they were doing well and a number had successfully escaped. How many survived the Civil Wars is another matter.

It is often overlooked that, quite aside from religious matters, one of the factors contributing to Charles I's downfall was his desperate and ill-advised attempt to resurrect the almost forgotten royal powers under the lapsed Forest Laws. By this means he attempted to extend the royal forest of Essex until almost the entire county was included, thus making the landowners virtually penniless and forcing Parliament to intervene in 1640 to annul these enlargements. By then Civil War was inevitable. Between 1642 and 1649 the Civil Wars caused enormous upheavals in the countryside, both in England and Scotland. The country was bitterly divided and both Cromwellians and Royalists plundered each other mercilessly. In the course of the struggle many estates were the scenes of minor battles and skirmishes. Numerous deer park walls were broken down and the deer themselves killed or scattered. Whether Cromwellian or Royalist, the troops on either side cared little for sporting rights. Deer were slaughtered with matchlock and wheellock muskets without much ado as to who owned them. At the start of the First Civil War there had been some seven hundred deer parks in existence, but by the end of the Second Civil War they had mostly been adversely affected to a greater or lesser degree and many had totally ceased to exist. The number of feral deer in the countryside must have been considerable.

By the return of Charles II at the Restoration in 1660 the countryside had changed irrevocably. The pace of the enclosures was quickening, the old forests were shrinking fast and the old aristocracy who had held sway over the countryside were giving way to the squires and the yeoman farmers who were to become the mainstay of sport in the countryside in the eighteenth century. Never-theless, this did not stop Charles II from importing 375 red deer in 1670 for release in the New Forest and it is indicative of the wide-spread poaching that had taken place that he needed to do so. It is interesting to note that the area of the New Forest then was assess-ed at around 92,000 acres (37,246 ha.), which is much the same as today.

What were the methods of shooting deer in the highlands at this time?

From eyewitness accounts during the seventeenth century, notably that of John Taylor in 1649, an unlikely highland traveller, Thames bargeman and rhymester, in his description of his journeys entitled *A Penniless Pilgrimage*, it appears that the old methods of hunting continued largely unchanged. The 'Tainchel', or deer hunt, was still conducted on similar methods to those used by the Saxons. Neighbouring clan chieftains would join together and a large area of the highlands would be driven to hunters waiting with deer hounds, guns, swords and bows and arrows. Several thousand deer would be driven to them and as many as four or five hundred killed, some to be feasted upon there and then while others were divided up amongst those engaged in the hunt.

Changes were taking place, however, and more of the old high-land forests were being cut down for charcoal so that whole areas were being totally denuded of trees at an alarming speed. There were, however, as yet no roads into the highlands and even to the Lowland Scot it was still largely unknown territory. The highland clansmen, wearing highland dress, speaking only Gaelic and totally isolated from contact with the south, were still regarded as uncivilised in garb and manners, little more than savages. The red deer by this time were mostly to be found beyond the highland line and only roe deer were to be found further south. Fallow deer were still virtually unknown in Scotland at this stage, despite James I and VI's introduction of some Norwegian fallow to the royal park at Dalkeith, which were subsequently sent to Epping Forest.

What were the chief changes in the highlands during the eighteenth century and their causes?

The Union of the Parliaments of England and Scotland in 1707 was to have far-reaching consequences, not least in providing the English with a source of previously unparalleled sport. The Jacobite uprising of 1715 resulted in the highlands being opened up for the first time by the construction of General Wade's military roads. Following the suppression of the uprising of 1745 the highlanders were subjected to extremely harsh laws forbidding the wearing of highland dress, the carrying of arms and similar oppressive restrictions which remained on the statute books for nearly forty years. The effect was to force many to join one of the eighty-odd highland regiments formed between 1730 and 1800, or else to emigrate overseas. Throughout the remainder of the century the highland glens and straths were gradually denuded of their human inhabitants. The highland chieftains, reduced in status to mere landlords, found that clansmen unable to pay any rent were merely a liability and tried at first to replace them with cattle. They also willingly sold off most of the remaining forests so that felling continued apace. Then in the last quarter of the eighteenth century sheep were introduced to the highlands and found to thrive profitably.

That disgraceful episode in highland history which followed, the forcible clearance of the highland glens, continued until well into the mid-nineteenth century, finally denuding the once populous highlands of humanity. The red deer, adapting themselves perforce to circumstances, learned to live on the bare mountain tops and higher glens where even the sheep could not survive. Yet the highlands themselves still remained virtually unknown save to a few intrepid explorers from the south, including the redoubtable Dr Johnson. The first man to write a book on the sporting possibilities of the highlands was an eccentric sporting squire from Yorkshire, Thomas Thornton, a Lt. Col. of the West Yorkshire Militia, who spent a decade or more in the 1780s visiting Speyside for the sport each season. At the turn of the century he published a book entitled *A Sporting Tour of the Highlands* covering his experiences of shooting grouse and ptarmigan and catching trout and salmon. It is an interesting point that he shot only one deer during this period and that was a roe.

It is surprising to realise that as late as 1800 the sport to be had from red deer stalking in the highlands was still completely unknown. Those deer that the highland chieftains wished to obtain for their own use were shot for them by their personal stalkers sent out explicitly to replenish the larder. Although Cluny Macpherson is reputed to have been the first man to stalk a deer on the open hill as early as 1747 after Culloden, this was a case of necessity. The chieftains themselves would have considered it beneath them to go out and stalk the deer personally and none of his peers for a century or more would have wished to emulate him. On the other hand, by the 1780s the tax on whisky distilling, about the only means of making highland farming pay at the time, was increased so much that the highlanders were forced to distil whisky illicitly to survive. From illegal whisky smuggling it can have been only a small step to poaching an occasional deer on the hills and many highlanders did not view it as a crime at all, but merely a way of providing their family with food during the winter months.

What was the general situation regarding deer in England and Wales during the eighteenth century?

During the eighteenth century foxhunting came into its own and became the leading English field sport indulged in by the majority of sporting squires to the exclusion of all else. For the first time hounds were bred specifically for the purpose of hunting one quarry. This did not mean to say, however, that there were not also quite a few packs of harriers hunting the hare, not to mention stag-hounds hunting the red deer and, of course, buckhounds hunting the fallow buck. The Royal Buckhounds started by William of Orange in 1703 had set a fashion and a number of packs of buck-hounds were formed in various parts of the country. Although it may have taken place occasionally in the New Forest and else-where, hunting the red deer seems to have been even then begin-ning to be concentrated chiefly in the West Country in the wild land around Exmoor.

With the development of an aesthetic taste for landscape garden-ing deer parks also became a feature of many country estates. The number which had increased from 32 in 1086, probably reached its peak of over 700 around the accession of Charles I, prior to the Civil War when many were destroyed. Then after the Restoration in 1660 the numbers began to build up again until by the year 1800 there were around 300. It is an interesting point that whereas they had previously been kept with a practical viewpoint in mind either to provide meat, or sport, they were now kept largely for aesthetic reasons to improve the view, or perhaps as an aristocratic version of keeping up with the neighbours.

The English cuisine, especially during the late eighteenth cen-tury was not calculated to make venison palatable. There were, of course, exceptions such as the Earl of Egremont at Petworth in Sussex who imported roe deer from Scotland and deliberately established them in his park around the end of the eighteenth century. Inevitably where one set an example it was copied by others, although in this instance apparently only in Dorset, where Lord Dorchester imported some roe from Perthshire and released them in his grounds at Milton Abbas. How many roe, if any, had survived from earlier introductions such as those of James I in the previous century is questionable. There were, however, still thriving herds of wild fallow deer to be found in various areas in the south as well as varied numbers of red deer in the remains of the old great forests such as Epping Forest, the New Forest, Cranborne Chase and in wilder places like Exmoor and of course royal parks such as Richmond and Windsor. Roe deer and red deer were still firmly established in Cumberland and roe deer were also common from Northumberland northwards.

Despite the increase in gamekeepers during the eighteenth century there is little doubt that deer poaching continued to be fairly widespread. The descriptions of such poaching in Cranborne Chase indicate that the poachers often went out equipped with sufficient to pay the fine on the spot should they be unfortunate enough to be caught. Although some were prepared to stalk and shoot their deer in the confines of the Chase in a sporting manner, others were not above driving them into nets and by any other form of poaching. No doubt poaching methods of similar kinds had been employed over the centuries from the days of the Normans and increasingly after the relaxation of the Forest Laws. It is only surprising in the circumstances that any deer of any sort remained and it is indicative of their ability to survive that they were still to be found, let alone poached, even in a fairly safe haven such as Cranborne Chase. It is ironic that the reason for the survival of the red deer and fallow deer over the centuries was basically that they were highly regarded from a hunting viewpoint and therefore preserved with care, while the roe deer, which had been relegated as an inferior beast of the warren, had by the eighteenth century been poached almost to extinction in most of southern England and was no longer to be found at all in Wales.

2

The Development of Deer Stalking in Britain from 1800

QUESTION AND ANSWER

What was the state of the highlands from 1800 to 1825?

As the remaining forests were cut down and as sheep grazed the mountainsides, the deer changed their habits and retreated to the high tops, while the remaining highlanders who had not emigrated or been forcibly removed in the Clearances, were also hard put to it to survive. One of the few means of making the subsistence farming on the fringes of the highlands profitable had been to distil the malted barley and produce whisky. By 1800 it was widely accepted that almost the only way to live in the highlands was by illicit distilling. It is no exaggeration to say that during the first quarter of the century illicit distilling was the main industry of the highlands. It was not until the law was revised in 1824 that it became possible to distil whisky legally and make a profit. Even then it took a further twenty-five years before illicit distilling ceased to be a problem of any magnitude.

In the circumstances it is small wonder that there were quite a few highlanders who were prepared to help themselves to deer in the remoter areas. Since men who outwitted the gauger (the exciseman), and delivered illicitly distilled whisky carried by packhorse across the mountains to willing recipients in the Lowlands were not regarded as criminals it is understandable that the killing of a few deer was not seen as much of a crime. That there were occasional outstanding figures amongst these largely nameless and unrecorded individuals is inevitable. Some even became minor folk lore heroes. Men like Alexander Davidson and John Farquharson spent much of their lives poaching deer and were in their way remarkable characters and even merited biographies. (See W. McCombie Smith, *The Romance of Poaching*, 1904)

How did such poachers stalk their deer?
The majority of the deer shot by such men were almost certainly seldom stalked in the modern manner, since the limitations of the

17

flintlock muzzle-loading guns of those days precluded anything
but very close-range shots. In general the poacher/stalker of those
days relied on taking up his position in some place he knew the
deer were likely to pass and taking his shot whenever the occasion
offered itself, allowing the deer to come to him rather than stalking
it in the accepted modern sense. Even so, this entailed a knowledge
of the hill and of the habits of the beasts, as well as considerable
stalking craft and hardiness, which many modern stalkers might be
hard put to emulate. It was indeed probably in a like manner that
the chieftain's chosen stalkers sent out to get venison for the table
completed their task.

Until the introduction of the percussion cap in the first decade of
the nineteenth century, attempting to shoot deer with a flintlock
gun in the mountains, especially in any sort of misty conditions,
must have been an extremely difficult business. It was perfectly
natural that the old chieftains regarded it as beneath their dignity to
go out and scramble round the mountains for little certainty of any
real reward. While they might be prepared to course a stag with
deer hounds in the old manner, quite understandably they did not
regard lying out on the hill to kill an occasional deer as sport. No
doubt some of the poachers too used deer hounds, or dogs of one
kind or another, to increase their chances of taking deer when only
wounded, but this was a reversion to older methods of taking deer.
The likelihood of being caught using such methods was of course
also far greater and anyone owning such dogs was likely to be a
marked man.

When did deer stalking in the modern sense start?

It is apparent from Thomas Thornton's book, *A Sporting Tour of the
Highlands*, that limited numbers of southern sportsmen were
coming up annually to the highlands for grouse shooting and fishing as early as the last quarter of the eighteenth century and there
are records of Lowland Scots leasing sporting ground on the fringes
of the highlands from 1800 onwards. It is questionable if either
grouse shooting or salmon fishing, in the highlands, began to
achieve much popularity until after Waterloo in 1815. With the
return to peace, books such as Thornton's, which although relating
to the 1780s was not published until 1804, and the enthusiastic
reports of other visitors, began to cause growing interest in the
sporting possibilities of the highlands. It was not until the 1820s
and '30s, however that real interest began to be shown and it is

questionable even then if many were interested in shooting deer. Sir Walter Scott's novels, the popularity of the highland regiments and the visit of George IV to Scotland, followed by the tartan revival, all helped to increase a general interest in the highlands. The opening of spas, such as those at Strathpeffer, close to Dingwall in Ross and Cromarty, and at Pananich, close to Ballater on Deeside, also helped to bring visitors to the highlands and increase this general interest.

It cannot really be said, however, that there was any great interest in deer stalking until, in 1839, William Scrope's book, *Days of Deer Stalking*, was published, the first of many on the subject. There is no doubt that this aroused considerable interest in the sport. Scrope's accounts of the methods employed stalking deer in Blair Athol and elsewhere were full of enthusiasm and racily written. The methods he recounted of using deer hounds may have been embroidered somewhat and he provided a good deal of extraneous folklore and anecdote, but he was still the first to write on stalking in the highlands and his book kindled the imagination of many sportsmen in the south. Then, in 1845, came Charles St. John's *Wild Sports and Natural History of the Highlands*, which ran into nine editions before the end of the century. He wrote of stalking deer, shooting and fishing as well as picturing the wild life he saw all round him in an easy and unaffected way which captured the interest of all who read him. From then onwards it is clear that deer-stalking became of increasing importance to the highland economy.

What effect did the establishment of the royal household at Balmoral have on the highlands and on stalking?

Victoria and Albert first visited the highlands in 1842 on what was in effect a delayed honeymoon and both fell under the spell of the highlanders and the highland scenery. In 1848 they first stayed at Balmoral and by 1850 they had bought it. It was with remarkable foresight that one observer of the scene, the Rev. Thomas McLauchlan, Gaelic scholar and Presbyterian minister, wrote in 1849:

> 'Much as we rejoice in our beloved Sovereign's visits to our country, we fear that they may hasten the consummation of making our Highlands a great deer forest by inducing a large number of our English aristocracy to flock to them for the purpose of sport.'

This, of course, is exactly what happened. It was ironic that around the 1840s and '50s it was discovered that grazing sheep on the hills could not continue indefinitely without turning the pasture sour. The sheep which had replaced the human inhabitants of the highlands were then in their turn replaced by the deer as Mr McLauchlan had foreseen.

Did the old method of deer hunting continue in the highlands at all during this transitional period?

It is apparent from Scrope's book that the Duke of Athol occasionally attempted deer driving with beaters and deer hounds to parties of guns waiting in suitable passes in the hills. At this stage deer hounds were also still used to follow up and bay stags that had only been wounded as all too often seems to have happened with muzzle-loading rifles. In some areas driving deer seems to have been continued even into the Edwardian era. The most outstanding example of deer coursing, however, took place in 1858, when Sir Samuel White Baker, author of *The Rifle and Hound in Ceylon,* was challenged to show his prowess in hunting a stag using only deer hounds and a knife. Unknowingly he had in fact revived the art of *par force* hunting in Ceylon and was accustomed to hunting deer on foot in this way. Using two deer hounds provided by the Duke of Athol, he coursed a stag in Glen Tilt in full view of a party of the Duke's guests and killed it in the river when the hounds brought it to bay. This was, however, a quite exceptional occasion.

Are there many game records of this transitional period?

At least one, the unpublished Game Records of Strathconan Estate dated 1841 and ending in the year 1850, still exists, covering exactly the transitional period when sheep were removed to make way for game and deer stalking began to develop in popularity.

Background
The 73,000 or so acres (29,554 ha) of Strathconan in Easter Ross, a little south of Strathpeffer were bought as a highland sporting estate in 1839 by Mr James Balfour of Whittingehame in East Lothian. It is significant that there was no mention of deer in the particulars of sale and the sheep were presumably cleared from it by 1841, the date on the front of the Game Book. Although thus prominently dated 1841, the first year entered is in fact 1842 and the year 1843 is not included, presumably because James Maitland Bal-

four, the heir to the estate, was married that year. The records for
the various years are as follows:

1842

Shooting began on the 13th of August and ended on the 26th
during which 505 grouse were shot over dogs. The total head of
game noted was 590, including thirty ptarmigan, fourteen black
game and four salmon, with no mention of either red or roe deer.

1844

The season ended on the 14th of September. On the 10th of August
Mr James Balfour went out and a note records: 'Shot a stag with 12
points and was going to cut his throat when he got up and ran off'.
On the 12th and 13th 136 grouse were shot over dogs. On the 14th
the first red deer was recorded and on the 16th another, but in
neither case are details of weight or the number of points on the antlers mentioned. On the 28th of August an entry reads; 'Mr
J. Balfour had a good shot at a stag but missed'. Another red deer
with no further details is recorded shot on the 31st and a fourth on
the 13th of September. Four red deer were thus included in the total
of 1,647 head of game shot, of which 1,510 were grouse.

1845

The season started on the 16th of August and ended on the 20th of
September. A red deer, with no further details given, is noted as
shot on the 19th. On the 30th of August a roebuck ·is recorded
without comment. The entry for the 6th of September notes: 'Saw 4
stags did not get a shot'. On the 8th of September: 'Got a shot at 2
stags: Talbot hit one and I think I wounded the other'. The total bag
recorded on the 20th of September was 1,723 head of which 1,552
were grouse with only the one red deer and the roebuck noted.

1846

James Balfour arrived on the 11th and caught a salmon, before
opening the grouse season on the 12th. The season ended on the
17th of September. Sandwiched amongst the records of the grouse
shooting are various notes on deer. On the 14th of August is recorded: 'Saw 6 stags and missed 2 shots'. On the 1st of September:
'Had a good chance at 5 stags' and without further details one red
deer is recorded killed. On the 2nd of September, apparently while
shooting grouse, 1 roe deer is also recorded. On the 5th of September: 'Missed 2 good stags: wounded another'. On the 10th, without
comment, another red deer is listed shot. On the 17th the season

ended with just the 2 red deer and the roe deer recorded in a total of 2,765 head shot of which, 2,395 were grouse.

1847

The shooting party appears to have arrived on the 10th of August and sport ended on the 29th of September. On the 11th of August is the laconic entry 'Wounded a stag'. On the 16th of August: 'Saw and missed 10 stags very fine. One a royal'. On the 23rd: 'A very fat stag killed by Sir I. Moncrieffe'. On the 26th another deer is recorded without comment. On the 2nd of September another is shot and the entry reads: 'Wounded 3 others'. On the 6th, 14th and 15th of September three further red deer are recorded but whether they are the three wounded is not recorded. The total is thus 6 red deer out of 1,145 head shot, of which 1,040 were grouse.

1848

The season opened on the 18th of August and finished on the 11th of October. There were only five days shooting in August and six in September so it may be assumed that this was an exceptionally wet year. On the 21st of September there is the cryptic entry: 'A hind by accident'. Compared with previous years this is by far the worst, with only 311 head shot, of which 239 were grouse and the hind represents the sole red deer.

1849

The season started on the 16th of August and ended on the 1st of October. The August 16th entry notes: 'Killed a number of old cocks: Saw a great many deer'. On the 21st: 'Saw about fifty deer'. On the 23rd the first is recorded without comment. On the 25th: 'Saw 3 deer but no shot'. On the 28th: 'Unlucky, I saw about 120 deer: 16 stone: 11 points'. On the 31st: 'The wind changed and spoiled our chances: saw a great many'. On 3rd Sept: 'Weight 13 st 3 lbs: 10 points'. On the 6th: 'Weight 10 st 11 lbs: 6 pts'. On the 7th: led our chances: saw a great many'. On 3rd Sept: 'Weight 13 st 3 lbs: 10 points'. On the 6th: 'Weight 10 st 11 lbs: 6 pts'. On the 7th: 'Weight 10 st 13 lbs: 7 pts'. On the 10th: '17 st 3 lbs: 9 pts'. On the 13th: '14 st: 9 pts'. On the 15th: 'Saw a good many deer, wind bad'. On the 18th: 'Saw a great many deer. Mr B. wounded a very good one'. On the 20th: '17 stone 8 lbs: 10 pts'. On the 21st: '14 stone 11 lbs: 12 pts'. On the 24th: 'The same stag as was wounded on the 18th: 18 stone 8 lbs: Points 12: Missed a stag, a long shot'. On the 26th: 'Missed a good chance'. On the 27th: 'Weight 12.6: Points 8'. On October 1st: 'Wounded a good stag'. Total for the season was

415 head which included 206 grouse and 7 salmon as well as 11 deer, including what appears to have been a good royal. The emphasis had now largely switched from grouse shooting to stalking and some good beasts had been recorded.

1850
The year starting on the 12th of August and ending on the 3rd of October reflects a similar continuing bias towards deer stalking. 12th August: '5 grouse: 2 deer: 10 pts. 13 stone 2 lbs'. On the 20th: '8 pts. 14 stone 7 lbs'. On the 22nd of August: '0'. On 27th: 'Three good chances'. On the 31st three roe deer were shot. On the 3rd of September: 'Missed a good chance'. On the 4th: '9 pts. 13 stone 5 lbs'. On the 5th: '10 pts. 9 stone 8 lbs. Hind. 9 stone 11 lbs'. On the 7th: 'Mr B wounded two good beasts and lost both: Two chances missed'. However, a roe deer was shot on the same day. On the 11th: 'Did not get a chance'. On the 13th: '8 pts. 12 stone 3 lbs'. On the 16th: '12 pts. 15 stone 6 lbs' and another roe was recorded. On the 19th: '6 pts. 11 stone 8 lbs; 11 pts: 17 stone 7 lbs'. On the 20th: 'Mr J. Balfour wounded 1'. on the 23rd: '10 pts. 15 stone 5 lbs'. On the 24th: '12 pts. 17 stone 8 lbs'. On the 25th: '12 pts. 18 stone 1 lb'. On the 26th: '11 pts. 14 stone 4 lbs'. On the 27th: '14 pts. 15 stone 12 lbs wounded on Sept. 7th'. On 3rd October: '9 pts. 15 stone 10 lbs'. The total bag for the year was 505 head; 266 grouse, 134 hares, 15 salmon, 5 roe deer and 16 red deer. The deer by this time were becoming the most important feature of the sport and to judge by the laconic comments some of the stags, including three royals and a fourteen-pointer, were of a very high standard.

Summary
By this time Mr James Balfour had died and this was probably the last year his son, James Maitland, visited the estate prior to his premature death after a seizure in 1854. Thereafter the estate was leased to sporting tenants until 1869, when Arthur James Balfour, James Maitland's eldest son, came of age and into possession of his estates. He was a keen deer stalker, but in 1885, owing to the widespread effects of the farming depression, he had to lease the estate again and finally sold it in 1891 to Mr R. Combe, whose family still own a large part of it. When A. J. Balfour sold it in 1891 it was noted as regularly providing the tenant with around 100 stags. This was rightly considered too many and was reduced to between seventy-five and eighty by the new owner.

The history of this area is thus typical of many in the highlands. Once quite well populated in the 1780s, the ground was then cleared for sheep. In 1839 these in turn were removed for sporting purposes and within a decade or so it had been turned into a deer forest. Similar far-reaching changes were taking place throughout the highlands. As the muzzle-loader gave way to the breech-loader in the 'sixties and 'seventies and as smokeless powder was introduced during the 'seventies and 'eighties the numbers of deer killed must have increased considerably. It is clear from these records, as well as from the early books on the subject, how many must have been wounded before it became possible to take a second shot without having the beast obscured by a cloud of black powder smoke.

What were the principal changes affecting deer in England in the nineteenth century?

Although red deer hunting continued in Exmoor this was the only part of the country where it really continued to flourish in the wild. Elsewhere, however, quite a number of packs of hounds were formed to hunt the carted red deer. These were fairly widely spread throughout southern England, the Midlands and East Anglia. The method involved keeping a number of deer in a park, acclimatising them and the hounds to each other, removing a stag's antlers before the hunt and then releasing the deer in the area to be hunted and giving it a few minutes 'law' before laying the hounds on the scent. Such deer frequently provided an excellent fast hunt, although without much hound work involved, and when closely pursued would generally take refuge in water, or stand at bay, while the hounds kept their distance. They could, however, only be used about three times a season, or they refused to run. The result was inevitably the spread of a few outliers from these hunts which had escaped the hounds completely. During the nineteenth century there appears to have been only one pack formed which specifically hunted roe deer, but there were a number of packs of buckhounds, particularly the Royal Buckhounds formed originally by William of Orange.

   Throughout the first half of the nineteenth century the stock of deer in the New Forest fluctuated between 4–8,000 and caused considerable damage to neighbouring estates and farmland. In the 1830s agitation caused the stock to be reduced to about 2,000, but it again increased beyond control and in 1851 the Deer Removal Act was passed with a view to killing all the deer in the Forest. For two years the deer were slaughtered by every means available, from

Roebuck alert to danger

organised driving, netting and shooting, to hunting with blood-hounds. By the end of two years all the red deer are thought to have been killed, but a number of fallow undoubtedly survived and once the Forest was peaceful again undoubtedly others returned. Throughout the century the number of deer parks had increased until by 1900 there were around 395 and there were, inevitably, a number of escapes which spread around the countryside. The centre for many of these was Woburn in Bedfordshire, where towards the end of the century fallow, sika and muntjac all escaped and established themselves in the wild.

What were the principal developments in the highlands in the latter half of the nineteenth century?

Undoubtedly the most obvious development in the highlands during the latter half of the nineteenth century was the acquisition of sporting estates by Englishmen and the building of shooting lodges. A considerable number of large granite buildings of Scottish 'baronial' style architecture, complete with turrets and crow-stepped gables, were erected in various unexpected parts of the country. By the end of the century a few of these lodges had been bought as investments by people who turned them into highland sporting hotels with salmon fishing and stalking available as attractions for their guests. Such as were successful, soon built up a regular clientele of retired Empire builders or similar sporting enthusiasts unable to afford a salmon river or 'deer forest' of their own, who annually returned to fish or stalk and in the evenings or on the Sabbath sat and read the bound copies of *Punch* accumulating in the smoking room with its comfortable leather bound arm-chairs. By the 1890s, with the development of rail travel, the highlands were much more readily accessible and the period from the 12th of August to around mid-October became the recognised period of annual migration when whole households moved from the south to the 'shooting lodge'. In the intervals, the highlands were almost deserted save for the stalkers in their isolated cottages, looking after the empty lodges and supervising the management of the estate.

How were the deer in the highlands affected in the latter half of the nineteenth century?
The new estate owners interested in increasing the head of deer available to shoot, as well as improving the growth of trophy ant-

lers, introduced the principle of feeding the deer in winter with imported hay and root crops. On the whole they also tended to introduce sound breeding principles by culling poor stock, such as hummels, or hornless stags, and encouraging the growth of good heads in every way they could. During the '70s and '80s a number of deer forest owners imported park deer from the south, but on the whole, although markedly superior in heads, such stock did not acclimatise readily to the conditions in the highlands and mostly died, or were shot on neighbouring ground, within a year or so.

During the '80s the American millionaire, Walter Winans, took over the sporting rights on nearly a quarter of a million acres of deer-stalking ground, as his favourite pastime was shooting driven deer on the move, at which he was a brilliant performer. He also did his best to improve the stock by every means available, but since he was directly responsible for a shortage of stalking ground over this period he was not popular. Another owner who frequently shot driven deer was the Duke of Fife, who owned a large acreage based on Mar Lodge, around the headwaters of the Dee.

During the '90s and in the first decade of the twentieth century one or two forest owners, including Winans, experimented with the introduction of fresh types of deer and at first sika and wapiti were tried, the latter in the hope of improving the heads. Although it seemed as if this ought to prove effective in producing larger trophy heads, in fact the reverse was found to be the case. Traces of wapiti influence were to be seen for several decades in areas where this was tried (as at Meoble, near Morar, for instance), but it was generally held to be unsuccessful. The sika also proved to be a not particularly successful introduction, since where they did cross with the red deer the heads were distinctly inferior and in general it was found they could not cope with the hard winters, although in some areas they established themselves reasonably successfully. A few deer forest owners in the southern highlands also encouraged the introduction of fallow deer. In certain parts of Perthshire fallow deer are still to be found, but they have never acclimatised in the highlands in the same way as red deer. Roe deer, on the other hand, are to be found in many areas and can provide good sport.

What were the principal changes in the Edwardian era?

One of King Edward VII's first actions was to bow to an outcry in the popular press against buck hunting by disbanding the Royal Pack of Buckhounds. On the other hand the Hon. Gerald Lascelles had formed the New Forest Buckhounds in 1883 and by the turn of the century they were flourishing as the numbers of deer, particularly fallow, but also red, continued to increase. Some were probably outliers from carted deer hunts, but others were probably deliberately released. One other survival of sport was notable in the highlands at Culachy, near Fort Augustus, where up to 1912 a Mr M. K. Angelo continued to course deer with deerhounds of his own breeding.

In that heyday of good living, stalking did not always require the considerable physical effort that is generally associated with it. King Edward VII, always a connoisseur of good living, who had been a keen stalker on the hill in his younger days, by the time of his accession was a corpulent *bon vivant*. His favourite method of shooting deer, like that of the Duke of Fife (who by the time he died had collected an amazing mausoleum of heads at Mar Lodge which may still be seen), was shooting them driven past him and was known to account for six with successive shots. Since the deer were passing quite close to his butt this is not, however, all that startling a feat. Nor was stalking on the hill necessarily arduous. At Meoble, for instance, wires had been laid to various vantage points on the mountains and under-stalkers were sent out to spend the night in the open. At dawn they would telephone in reports of the best stags to be seen in their vicinity and the state of the wind and the weather. The head stalker, acting on this information, would then retrieve the guests of the day from the breakfast room where they had consumed an ample breakfast, followed by champagne, and mount them on ponies which would carry them to suitable positions for a picnic lunch and more champagne, close to where the deer had been seen. After another shorter ride, they would then dismount and follow the stalker to a pre-arranged point where they would be handed the rifle, take their shot and either kill, or miss, their stag. Without further ado they would then return to the lodge on horseback, smoking a choice Havana, ready for a five- or six-course dinner to recover from their exertions.

While not all deer forests in the Edwardian period carried matters to quite these extremes, there is no doubt that many elderly sportsmen found little need to exert themselves and in general the standard of sportsmanship as well as marksmanship seems to have been extremely low according to many records of the time. Inevitably in a period when money counted for little, more experiments with the introduction of wapiti, sika and park-bred deer were tried. Experiments were also made with fencing in attempts to enclose whole deer forests, but in general these proved to be unsuccessful and were widely regarded as unsporting.

What were the effects of the First World War 1914–1918?

Although many deer were poached in deer parks and estates throughout the country, many others, both red and fallow, escaped into the wild and established themselves in suitable areas. It was certainly not shortage of red deer which caused the New Forest Deerhounds to change their name early in the War to the New Forest Buckhounds. By the end of the war the deer population in many areas was a good deal larger than it had been, since the keepers and others who might have kept them under control had been away. This was also the case in the highlands where, on the whole, no real attempt to cull suitable numbers had been possible. After the war the break up of many of the old estates also led to considerable reduction in the number of deer parks with, in some cases, the deer escaping to add to the number of feral beasts.

One of the most important side-effects of the war, however, was probably the formation of the Forestry Commission in 1919. In 1923, by the Forestry Act, the Crown's interest in the New Forest was vested in the Forestry Commission. Although no doubt it seemed a good idea at the time to ensure timber stocks in the event of any future war, the formation of this giant state monopoly, lacking real control, or often, it must have seemed, real purpose, was to become a source of considerable irritation to landowners as well as cause concern to all those interested in deer. Especially during the period between the two world wars the Commission waged continual war on deer, using shotguns and rifles, in or out of season, with a view to protecting young plantations. At this time they had no interest in the sporting or naturalist aspects of forestry and like many faceless government departments of the period saw no value in publicity. They saw no need to explain their actions and rode roughshod over any landowners unable or unwilling to take legal action against them.

When were Firearms Certificates introduced?
Perhaps one of the more important, if indirect, side effects of the First World War on deer stalking was the 'temporary' introduction of the Firearms Certificate required by those who wished to possess a rifled firearm. Like so much wartime legislation, intended merely to cover the period of 'hostilities only', this was never repealed.

Although shotguns were not affected, it became necessary for anyone owning a rifle to register with the police and obtain a Certificate. After the war, since there was insufficient outcry against it, the legislation was left unaltered on the familiar grounds of 'public order'. Thus, anyone wishing to own a rifle had first to approach the local police force and establish himself as of good character and having good reason for requiring a rifle. It was no longer possible simply to walk into a gunsmith and choose a rifle and ammunition for stalking, rabbit shooting, or big game hunting.

Inevitably this led in course of time to a natural inertia amongst those who did not own a rifle, or have any immediate requirement for one. They did not buy one because of the small but irksome necessity of applying for a licence. In a small way, over the ensuing years, this probably helped to restrict the number of people who might otherwise have found an interest in deer stalking. Those who went stalking for the first time usually borrowed a rifle for the purpose, even if by doing so they were, in fact, breaking the law. Although it was not intended to do so the Act inevitably tended to make deer stalking less widely available and less attractive to many who might otherwise have been interested.

What were the main changes in the overall picture in the '20s and '30s?

In England the number of hunts was considerably reduced. There were fewer packs of buckhounds and also fewer hunting the carted stag. Red deer were still hunted on Exmoor, where the terrain was particularly suited to this form of sport. There were still around two hundred or so parks holding either red or fallow deer in England and Wales, but this was well down on the pre-war figures. Stalking deer was still regarded as something conducted only in the highlands. If deer were to be shot in the wild anywhere else it was usually only by an organised drive where shotguns were used, resulting generally in numbers of wounded deer and almost always a somewhat grisly business.

What were the effects of the Second World War from 1939–45?

Once again the country was involved in a life or death struggle during which the large estates were mostly doing their best to produce as much food as possible to beat the U-boat blockades. Most deer parks were affected to a considerable extent and the deer were either slaughtered, poached, or escaped. Once again the deer in the highlands increased considerably in numbers owing to lack of ammunition, or people, to cull them properly. Despite a good deal of poaching the same was probably true of the wild deer population throughout most of England, for there were large areas such as ammunition dumps, the edges of airfields, army camps and similar rough patches eminently suitable for deer, where those who might have culled them were unable to obtain access. This was not the case with the Forestry Commission areas, but in general their efforts to cull deer at this stage were inefficient in the extreme, still relying chiefly on deer drives with shotguns.

What was the situation in the post-war period of the '50s?

The last of the carted deer hunts finally gave up in this period and deer hunting with hounds was restricted to the pack of the New Forest Buckhounds and in the West Country to the Devon and Somerset Staghounds and the Tiverton Staghounds, which were pre-eminently placed to conduct their sport in surroundings where it was both suitable and desirable. It was, for instance, obvious during the war and shortly afterwards that any time the Devon and Somerset were for one reason or another unable to hunt, poaching of deer with shotguns and the consequent wounding and maiming of deer was the immediate result. In the highlands the scale of poaching from roadsides by organised gangs of criminals eager to supplement the meagre post-war meat rations in the black market caused action to be taken by Parliament and the Deer (Scotland) Act was introduced in 1952, although only finally passed in 1959. The Act had five parts: I. Conservation and Control of Red Deer. II. Close Seasons. III. Prevention of Illegal Taking and Killing of Deer. IV. Enforcement and Procedure. V. Supplementary. To enforce Part I, a Red Deer Commission was formed with power to require any landowner, or occupier, to supply a return of deer of each sex killed. Where necessary they might also authorise deer to be killed. A Close Season was enforced: for stags from 21st October to 30th June: for hinds, from 16th February to 20th October.

The return of many ex-servicemen who had learned to use a rifle on the continent and experienced the high degree of conservation there resulted in the formation of the Deer Group of the Mammal Society, which started to try to educate public opinion by producing informative booklets on deer. Meanwhile the Forestry Commission continued to expand the acreage under its control. By the Forestry Act of 1948 the Crown interest in the New Forest was vested in the Minister of Agriculture and entrusted to the Forestry Commissioners under his control. Elsewhere in the country the Commission continued to take over great tracts of frequently excellent farming land for forestry and despite swelling opposition continued the policy of deer drives.

What were the principal changes in the 1960s?

One of the most important features of the 1960s was the Deer Act of 1963, which saw important innovations affecting deer in England, providing close seasons for them and increased powers of dealing with offenders under it, also defining Prohibited Firearms and Ammunition.

The main clauses in the 1963 Act were in effect:

1 A Game Licence is required to shoot deer.
2 *a*. If a shotgun is used it must be loaded only with S.S.G.
  b. If a rifle is used it must have a calibre of .240 or over and a muzzle energy of not less than 1700 foot pounds and fire a soft-nosed, or hollow-nosed, bullet.
3 Unless marauding crops on enclosed land, deer may only be shot from one hour before sunrise to one hour after sunset, but they may be shot on Sunday.

Close Seasons were introduced, but did not include roe, nor did they coincide with those of Scotland, introduced under the Deer (Scotland) Act. Another important feature of 1963 was the formation of the British Deer Society, formed from the Deer Group of the Mammal Society, for the study of deer and dissemination of knowledge for scientific and educational purposes.

By this time around 150 of the pre-war deer parks had gradually been replaced, but fallow deer had established themselves in the wild throughout a great part of England. Escaping muntjac and Chinese water deer had also established themselves within a forty- or fifty-mile radius of Woburn. Sika had established themselves in isolated pockets around the country and roe deer were making a steady return, spreading through many areas in the south, especially around Sussex and Surrey, as well as in Dorset, Hampshire and Wiltshire down to Devon.

One innovation which by this time was coming into general use was the telescopic sight on rifles, which had hitherto been too expensive to be widely used.

What were the principal changes in the '70s and '80s?

In the deer forests ponies were giving way to tracked and four-wheel-drive vehicles and even helicopters in places. Modern technology was being introduced into the highlands at last. The use of two-way radios was superseding such time-honoured if effective methods as lighting a small fire to attract the attention of the pony man.

With the prompting of the Deer Society and the Red Deer Commission further legislation was introduced through Parliament. For the first time some sensible and humane legislation regarding deer was passed. Even so it was 1977 before Close Seasons for deer were finally introduced as follows:

In England:
    Red and Sika deer: Stags: 1st May–31st July: Hinds: 1st March–31st October.
    Fallow Deer: Bucks: 1st May–31st July: Does: 1st March–31st October.
    Roe deer: Bucks: 1st November–31st March: Does: 1st March–31st October.

In Scotland:
    Red, Sika, or Hybrids: Stags: 21st October–30th June: Hinds: 18th February–20th October.
    Fallow deer: Bucks: 21st October–31st July: Does: 18th February–20th October.
    Roe deer: Bucks: 21st October–30th April: Does: 1st April–20th October.
    Recommended Close Season for muntjac and Chinese water deer, both Bucks and Does: 1st March–11th October (but this is not yet law).

By this time the telescopic sight was in common use and even the Forestry Commission had been forced to change its old methods. Under the prompting of public opinion a revolution had quietly taken place in the late '60s and early '70s. After many years of ignoring the general public it now began to attend to its public relations, making its forests as far as possible attractive to the public, varying their forestry when possible, and appointing individual stalkers properly trained and equipped with suitable rifles to control the deer in given areas. By the '80s, however, the pointlessness of growing much more timber was apparent and large areas were being sold off to private enterprise. Even so the Forestry Commission remains by far the largest landowner in the country as well as controlling very considerable sporting rights.

Throughout this period the costs of all forms of stalking rose as other members of the Common Market and the North Americans became aware of what was available here, not merely in the highlands, but also in woodland stalking throughout the country. Like the costs of all other field sports it seems almost certain to continue to rise. Stalking remains, however, one of the comparatively undervalued field sports in many places and for the keen stalker there is always the great advantage in that shooting deer is by no means the ultimate satisfaction involved.

3

The Deer

TERMINOLOGY, DESCRIPTION, HABITS,
HABITAT AND DISTRIBUTION

Part I

Common Factors

Common factors and preliminary points

There are certain points which all, or most, of the species of
deer found in the U.K. share in common, as for instance the fact
that, apart from the comparative newcomer, the Chinese water
deer, the sexes are immediately distinguishable by the fact that
the males grow antlers, while the females, with rare exceptions,
do not.

Antler growth and terminology

As noted, apart from the Chinese water deer, all male deer grow
antlers, not horns. These antlers are **cast**, or shed, annually and re-
growth usually starts at once. Most species have definite periods
when the antlers are cast, or dropped, and only the muntjac, those
other comparative newcomers, are exceptional in that they are
liable to cast their antlers at any time of the year. The growing antlers start as small knobs on a part of the skull on either side known
as the **pedicle**, on top of which is formed the **coronet**, or **burr**, at the
base of the antlers. The growing antlers are covered with a soft and
sensitive skin, composed of hair and blood vessels and are then
known as being **in velvet**. The velvet covers the antlers until they
are fully grown and the soft horn underneath has hardened. When
this happens the blood vessels close, the velvet dries and starts to
irritate, and is then rubbed off on trees, stones, or bushes. This is
known as **fraying** and when the antlers are free of velvet they are
said to be **clean**. Generally the antlers will increase in size annually
until the animal is said to be **in its prime**, then they will start to deteriorate and may be said to be **going back**.

Eating habits

All deer cut their food with the lower incisor teeth against a hard pad of flesh in the upper jaw and grind their food with their cheek

Roe deer in u

teeth. Like all ruminants they have four chambers in the stomach. During feeding the first of these, the rumen, is filled so that while resting in cover later the animal can regurgitate a cheekful of food,

the doe's rump patch as shown is distinguished by the tail which the buck lacks

known as the cud, and chew it slowly some sixty times before swallowing and starting the process of digestion in a second chamber, the reticulum. The cheek is then re-filled preparatory to ruminating again until the digestive process is complete.

Deer are both grazers, eating herbage of all kinds, as well as browsers, eating leaves and stripping branches of trees and bushes. Although most deer tend to eat primarily at dawn and dusk, they will also eat through the night if circumstances are favourable, as when there is a full moon. Where undisturbed, however, they may also eat freely during the day, although they tend to lie for considerable periods chewing the cud.

Food
Their choice of food depends a great deal on their environment, but can be extremely varied. Where open litter bins are to be found on picnic sites, for example, they will sometimes nose through them and eat almost anything from stale ham sandwiches to the plastic bag in which they were wrapped. On farm land they will graze pastures, often damaging growing hay, or young cereal crops such as wheat and barley. They will also eat ears of grain, but probably do more damage to crops by lying up in them and trampling them to get at the vegetation and grasses underneath. They will also eat most root crops, such as sugar beet, mangolds, turnips, swedes, carrots and potatoes and, of course, find cabbages or similar vegetables very attractive. As they are principally grazing animals, grasses, particularly the sedges, herbs, lichens, mosses and fungi, fruits and shrubs form a large part of their diet. Bracken and ferns are also eaten, especially when young. Brambles, wild roses, heather and gorse shoots are also eaten freely and deer will even eat holly, ivy and green yew in winter time. Bilberries, blackberries, wild strawberries and raspberries, crab apples, sweet chestnuts, beech mast and acorns will all be eaten in season if available.

Damage caused
As noted, deer can cause varied damage to farm crops. Unfortunately they are also browsers and will eat most broad-leafed trees, such as oak, elm, beech, poplar and sweet chestnuts, as well as most conifers. In some regular feeding areas the browse-line amongst the trees may be indicative of the size, sex and age of an individual, or the species of deer concerned. They will also eat the bark of holly, yew, cypress, spruce and pine amongst others. This is known as **stripping**. They may also damage trees and bushes by

fraying when cleaning their antlers of velvet, or marking out their territories, or just in play. The damage deer may cause to forestry can thus be considerable, although by sensible planting methods it can usually be minimised.

The difference between the damage caused to seedling trees by a hare and by deer, especially roe, is often difficult to distinguish at first sight, but on close examination the bite of a hare will be seen to be absolutely clean, as if with a knife, while that of the deer will show a very slight ragged nibbling effect. Damage to forestry is often blamed on the wrong culprit by those who have failed to examine it closely enough.

Eyesight, hearing and scenting abilities

Deer have large eyes and are good at noticing movement, or anything unusual, although not apparently able to distinguish objects clearly, as for instance a stalker against a bush, or behind a tree or boulder. They also have a tendency not to look upwards, so that observers in trees in woodland, or on hillsides above them in the open, are not so likely to be seen as someone on their own level, or below them. Their ears are large and constantly moving, able to pick up sound at a considerable distance. They all have strong scenting powers, able to scent humans at a considerable distance, even up to half a mile or more in the open. Their scenting abilities are also used when checking territorial boundaries and when roused sexually. When feeding they are constantly raising their heads and looking round them alertly, checking the wind for scent and using their ears to detect any unusual sound. In woodland surroundings they tend to rely on hearing and scent rather than sight, and on absolute stillness, or creeping silently through undergrowth, to avoid detection, prior to outright flight when thoroughly disturbed. In the open they tend to lie in such a position that the wind will bring them the scent of any danger approaching them from the rear, while their ears and eyes cover the approach of any enemy from the front and sides.

Ageing

Depending on the species, the size and shape of the antlers should give an indication of the deer's age, but factors such as feeding, accidents and severe winters can affect this considerably and it can only be an indication. The general appearance of the deer is a more reliable indicator of age. The young are clearly more lightly built, upright and alert but full of curiosity. After a few years they are more obviously filled out, muscled and apprehensive of danger. As they grow older the head carriage is noticeably lower and the body generally more thickset. They are generally very shy and liable to be alone. The very old deer has an extremely low head carriage and shows loss of condition and stiffness of movement.

It is only by experience that it is possible to make an estimate of a deer's age and even then it is very easy to be mistaken. The wear on the teeth can be an accurate method of ageing, but, of course, the deer must be dead or unconscious for this method to be employed.

Scent glands

Most species have various scent glands, although these are often barely discernible. They are usually either:
a. interdigital: between the cleaves of each foot;
b. metatarsal: just below the hock on the outside of each hind leg;
c. suborbital: just below the corner of each eye.
There may also be scent glands in the sheath of the penis and in the region of the vulva, or anus, active during the rut.

The scent glands are utilised in marking territories and have special significance during the rut, although their purposes and functions are by no means fully understood.

Part II

Red deer: *Cervus elaphus*

Terminology

The male is known as a **stag**. The term hart, common in hunting from the days of the Normans, is now very rarely used. The female is known as a **hind**, never a doe. A hind which has not bred is known as a **yeld hind**, but is not necessarily barren. The young of both sexes are known as **calves**, never as fawns. The period of the mating season in the autumn is known as the **rut**. The stag sheds his antlers annually in the spring and re-grows them by the late summer. Antler growth is generally predictable except in the case of an injured stag. In their second year male calves grow a small knob under the dark velvet on each side of their head and in the highlands are known as **knobbers**. At the same stage on Exmoor and in southern parks they are known as **prickets**. In the third year the calf grows small antlers and in the highlands is then known as a **staggie**, or more correctly perhaps as a **brocket**. From six years of age the staggie may correctly be termed a stag, for he will by then be more or less fully grown, although his antlers will still be very light. By then he may have seven or eight **points** and if nothing else is available may be considered shootable, but by eight years he should be in his prime and from then on to thirteen or fourteen years he may attain a full head of twelve points, known as a **royal**, if he is going to do so.

After fourteen years he will probably start to deteriorate and lose points. From this stage onwards he may be termed an old stag going back and should be culled if possible. Some stags do not grow antlers and are known as **hummels** in the highlands, or on Exmoor as **notts**. They are usually very large beasts, since all their food intake goes towards body growth and not into antler growth. They should be culled whenever possible.

Antler growth and terminology

The stag's antlers are shed annually and the growth takes only four or five months. It usually starts in late April when the antlers are cast and by late August the antlers have attained full growth. From the coronet, or burr, stems the main shaft, or **beam**. The **tines**, or points, projecting from the beam above the burr are known as the **brow** tines, above them are the **bay** tines, or anciently bez, and above them the **tray** tines, or anciently trez. Any points branching from the beam above the trays are called the **points on top**. A stag with twelve points in all, brows, bays, trays and points on top, including three on each top preferably, but not necessarily, forming a cup, is known as a royal.

Any stag with less than twelve points is known by the number of points, i.e. a ten-pointer. A head with an uneven number may be upgraded one with the prefix 'uneven', i.e. an uneven twelve-pointer. Beyond a royal a stag should again be known by the number of points, i.e. a thirteen-, or sixteen-pointer. A fourteen-pointer is sometimes referred to as an **imperial**, but there seem no good grounds for doing so. Park deer and those in Thetford Chase may show eighteen or twenty points upwards and some especially well fed Continental deer have been known to have over forty. When the antlers have been damaged in velvet, or the stag itself has been injured, freak heads may result. A quite common occurrence

also is that known as a **switch**, or switch head, when there are only
four points, beam and brow only, or just two points, beam only. As
with hummels, these should be culled whenever possible, since it is
not desirable to perpetuate such heads, particularly as they are very
lethal and liable to kill other and better stags during the rut.

Description

Heights and weights
The species *Cervus elaphus* is the largest British deer, with slender
legs and well shaped cloven hooves, reddish brown coat, powerful
body and rump with a tufted tail about six inches (15 cm) long, a
neat head, alert dark brown eyes and large ears. In their habitat
amongst the highland mountains they present a picture of cervine
beauty which has attracted many artists. They do, however, vary
greatly in size and weight, as do the appearance, shape and size of
the antlers on the male. Some naturalists have insisted that they
should be divided into sub-species, classifying Scottish red deer as
Cervus elaphus scoticus, but on the whole the chief difference between a park-fed deer in the south of England, or a red deer in say
Thetford Chase, compared with a wild highland deer, is usually
little more than that of size and weight, due almost entirely to available feeding. When full grown the average highland stag will stand
from 40 to 45 inches (101–114 cm) at the shoulder, weighing from 14
to 16 stone (88–102 kg). The greatest weights that have been known
in the highlands are around thirty stone (190 kg), but any stag
weighing twenty stone (126 kg) would be considered a very outstanding weight for a stag on the hill.

The hind is smaller and more lightly built and, of course, is
without antlers, although hinds with antlers have been known.
The average height of a hind is between 38 to 42 inches (96–104 cm)
at the shoulder and the weight around 8 to 11 stone (50–70 kg).
Sometimes, of course, heavier beasts may be encountered, but
never anything approaching a full grown stag. A park-fed stag may
stand from 42 to 50 inches (107–127 cm) at the shoulder and weigh
as much as 16 to 25 stone (102–158 kg). The hinds will generally
stand from 3 to 5 inches (7–13 cm) less at the shoulder and weigh
correspondingly less. Weight is generally measured in **clean
weight**, i.e. with the stomach, bowels, intestines and lungs removed and only the heart, liver and kidneys left in the body, but
there are local variations as to exactly what should be left to consti-
tute clean weight.

Colour and coat

In summer the red deer's normal coat is a short and reddish brown with a thick grey undercoat, but there are considerable variations through dark red to brown or buff. In the winter the coat becomes rougher and thicker and turns a greyish brown, growing gradually greyer until in the spring after rolling in peat hags it is finally cast. Stags may roll in peat hags at any time and are sometimes then termed black, but real melanistic coats, or for that matter white deer, are very uncommon, although a white face, or blaze, as on a horse, known as a bald face, is not uncommon in some places. The stags also have a ridge of coarse long hair along the spine and on the neck. During the rut, or mating season, this becomes a mane, which can be a formidable spectacle. As the stag grows older the mane is retained throughout the year, but when younger it is for the most part lost with the spring change of coat.

Age and teeth

Red deer have a generally estimated life span of around fifteen years and anything beyond that is exceptional. After a series of severe winters the more probable life expectancy may well be nearer twelve or so. Visual evidence of ageing is shown by the size and growth of the deer, but it can only provide a rough estimate. A three- or four-year-old stag will have a noticeably long face, no dewlap and virtually no mane and the rump will be sloping. A five- or seven-year-old stag will have a noticeable dewlap and mane and a noticeably fuller body with a rounded rump. An old stag will have a prominent dewlap and mane, a heavy body with prominent withers and a strong rump and hindquarters. Because the food is ground by the molars in the cheek the wear on these is a means of assessing age. By around the thirtieth month the milk teeth will have been replaced by adult teeth which are very sharp. The chewing surfaces wear with age and by eight years they will be almost smooth and showing signs of wear. Decay usually sets in by around fourteen.

Gait and agility

They have all the gaits of a horse, the walk, the trot, canter and gallop and when necessary they can keep up a fast speed for miles. Their most characteristic gait is probably a dignified trot with the head erect and steady. They can also swim extremely well and when closely pursued by hounds will usually take to water, covering considerable distances. Stags have been known at times to swim between adjacent islands off the coast of Scotland during the rut and on the mainland may often travel for considerable distances at this time. Their agility is also considerable and they can leap deer fences over six feet high (183 cm) with comparative ease, as well as squeezing through remarkably narrow gaps in fences, or similar obstacles when they require to do so. They are also extremely surefooted and are seldom known to slip on mountain slopes unless harried by predators such as men or dogs, or on occasions eagles.

Slots and droppings
The footprint, or **slot**, is large and the width at the heel is about 2½ inches (6 cm). The step is about 24 inches (60 cm) when walking normally. The fore and hind slots resemble each other. The marks of the dew claws are prominent at speed.

The droppings are lightish brown to black and acorn-shaped, fitting into each other and sometimes adhering. In August and September when the stag is fat before the rut they may be soft and look like small cow pats.

Powers of scent, eyesight, hearing and voice
Red deer have remarkably fine powers of scent and are capable of scenting man at a distance of hundreds of yards downwind in normal conditions, but their eyesight, although quick to pick up any movement, is not particularly keen, especially at distinguishing objects which are not moving, e.g. stalkers in full view lying quite still amongst broken ground. Their hearing, however, is acute and when looking at any object of which they are suspicious their ears will be cocked alertly, focusing all their auditory powers. They tend to lie with the wind at their backs so that they can scent danger approaching from behind and see and hear danger approaching from the front. When lying in any sort of cover, especially amongst trees, they tend to rely on remaining absolutely still to avoid discovery even when danger is close at hand. On the whole they seldom look upwards, hence on the hill it is always advisable to try to stalk deer from above whenever possible. Although normally silent, both stag and hind may give a gruff warning bark on scenting danger. The hind, as noted, bleats to call the calf and the stag bellows, or 'roars' during the rut. Woodland stags may also groan at intervals.

Habits

Relationships and social behaviour

Red deer are gregarious, but except during the rut the stags live apart from the hinds. In mid-November after the rut the hinds gather together in herds of from ten upwards to fifty or more, with the calves of the year and of the previous year at foot, ranging their usual territory. They are usually led by an old hind and there is a fairly strict order of precedence in the matriarchal group.

When fresh antler growth has begun, the stags will usually leave for higher ground, if possible, where they tend to gather in groups of from three or four to as many as twenty or thirty, until re-growth is over and they are clear of velvet. It is not usually long then until the rut, when the stags start challenging each other and collecting the hinds in harems around them. A master stag will then collect a small herd of hinds around him along with their calves. In some cases the velvet may not have been cleared when the rut starts, in which case of course a stag still tender in late velvet is at a very great disadvantage compared with even a smaller beast whose antlers are hard and clear of velvet. Prior to the rut, however, there is usually a period of peace when the stags are clear of velvet, but not yet in rut. Then three or four stags may be found together, or very often a mature beast may pair with a young indifferent stag, which is then known as its **fag**, on whom it relies for warning of danger while it feeds. Studies on the Isle of Rhum have shown that although a two- or three-year-old staggie might be capable of covering a hind it is not generally sexually mature until about seven years, but this is a limited community and on the mainland where there is a preponderance of hinds it might be different.

Feeding

Like most deer, red deer feed principally at nightfall and at dawn, or through the night if conditions are suitable for them, although they may frequently also be seen grazing, or browsing, at intervals during the day if nothing has disturbed them. When lying down and resting they will chew the cud. They will graze on grass, herbs, lichens and young heather tops where they are available. They will also browse noisily on leafy branches of bushes and trees, which they will pull down from a height of six feet. If there are any crops of roots, or growing corn, within range of their feeding grounds they will often do considerable damage to them, hence they tend to be unpopular with foresters and farmers. Island deer, or those living within range of the sea-shore will often be seen eating sea-weed. They will also eat discarded antlers and any bones they may encounter, for their salt content. They are also sometimes flesh eaters, given the opportunity, and may be seen eating occasional carrion, or animals such as rabbits caught in traps. Like most deer, as indicated they will eat almost anything, including the contents of litter bins where available.

Gestation, birth and growth of calf
The period of gestation is around seven or eight months and the calves are usually dropped around the end of May or early June. Twins are very rare, but are known to occur. The birth is usually very quick and the hind will generally remain standing throughout it. The calf is about the size of a hare and its coat is spotted, although as the winter coat grows these spots disappear. The calves are secreted in patches of cover such as heather, or bracken, or in a hollow amongst boulders, and the hind returns to them to suckle them. They will not stir for the first week, lying stretched out like a hare in its form, motionless and blending almost perfectly with the background. During this period, however, they are often prey to foxes, or eagles, although of the two the fox is by far the more dangerous predator. After about three weeks the calves are able to follow their mothers and the hinds are usually careful and protective, keeping up a fairly continuous fussing, calling them with a rather scolding bleat which is answered by a plaintive, much higher pitched, bleat.

By the time they are two months old the calves are becoming strong and playful and by the time they have survived to three months they are more or less safe from most danger. It has been estimated, however, that mortality can be as high as thirty per cent. They will, however, tend to be reliant on mother for their first year and frequently stay on with her even when there is another calf at foot. Indeed it is quite common to see a yearling calf, although well able to provide for itself, still suckling from its mother occasionally.

The rut
The rut usually begins about the middle of September and continues until the end of October. The mating fever grips the stags and they begin to fight and challenge each other. Each stag that is mature enough to hold his own sets out to collect as many hinds as he can and defends them against any others. All other males are

driven away, excepting calves and knobbers, and he will round up any stragglers from his harem of hinds like a sheepdog, doing his best to remove any he can from other herds without losing any of his own. Since, during the rut, the stags roar extremely loudly and their manes are often very pronounced this adds a distinctly leonine flavour to the proceedings. The deep rutting roar tends to peter out in a series of deep coughs, but it is still an impressive sound, especially in approaching darkness or misty conditions. A large stag with a sizeable harem of hinds will be kept very busy preventing lesser beasts from abstracting any of them and in the course of the rut it is understandable that they become very run down and out of condition. Very often one or two lesser stags may then take over the herd and the master-stag may be forced to retire. The hinds, being polyandrous, do not seem to feel partiality for any particular stag.

Movements and range
In the highlands red deer normally move in single file over recognised routes in the hills. Such deer passes are usually well worn, like sheep tracks. Acquaintance with all of the commoner ones on his ground is a valuable and necessary part of any stalker's knowledge and can often be put to good use when deer are seen to be moving away, since it may well be possible to take a short cut and be waiting for them in a suitable position. The hinds will usually lead when deer are moving and the old hinds are particularly observant and wary of danger. The stags will usually bring up the rear of any mixed group. Only when thoroughly alarmed are red deer likely to bunch and gallop off upwind from the source of their fright.

They are also a useful barometer of bad weather and may be seen to move off exposed high ground when storms are approaching. They are seldom caught in snowdrifts as they usually prefer to stay on windswept ground in bad weather. In the heavy winters, of course, they are forced to come down to lower ground in search of food. During the rut, stags are known to travel distances of fifteen miles or more.

Habitat
Red deer are naturally beasts of the forest. In Exmoor they tend to inhabit the forest land and steep-sided rough combes with thickly wooded bottoms. In Thetford Chase they are completely at home. In the Lake District and Cumbria and more especially in the high-

lands of Scotland they have been forced by the gradual loss of their natural habitat to adapt to a more unnatural existence on the bare mountainsides. Hence these barren, rocky areas of mountain have been termed deer forests even though in many instances there is no trace of any trees to be seen. In both forms of habitat, however, the stags enjoy nothing better than the chance to wallow in a peat hag, or muddy pool, particularly during hot weather. Especially in forested areas it is often possible to judge the age, size, numbers and even the quality of deer by their slots in the neighbourhood of such muddy ground.

Distribution

In England red deer are to be found in considerable numbers on Exmoor in Devon and Somerset, as well as in Cumbria in the Lake District. Smaller numbers are present in the wild in East Anglia, in Thetford Chase, in Hampshire, in the New Forest, in Sussex and in Staffordshire. In Scotland they are present in all counties north of the Highland Line. They are also to be found in Ayrshire and Kirk-cudbrightshire, as well as on fourteen islands off the mainland.

Part III

Roe Deer: *Capreolus capreolus*

Terminology

The male is known as a **buck**, not a stag. The female is known as a **doe**, not a hind. The young of both sexes are known as **kids**, or **fawns**, although the former is probably more correct. They should not, however, be termed calves. As with red deer, antlers on a doe are not unknown, if very uncommon.

Antler growth and terminology

The buck sheds his antlers annually from mid-October to mid-November and they start re-growing at once, being usually free of velvet by March or April. Unlike the red deer no two pairs of roe antlers are alike, although the rate of growth is generally predictable, save, once again, in the case of an injured beast. The kids are born in May, or early June, and the male kid starts growing vestigial antlers at about the age of three months with the growth of the pedicles. By November the pedicles are covered with soft gristly tops, known as **buttons**, which are rubbed off in February. Then the first antlers grow as small bony **spikes** in velvet. The velvet is shed in early June by the youngster fraying on young saplings, or bushes. These spikes are usually cast after the older bucks, but thereafter the second head of antlers starts growing at once. This usually starts with bony mounds covered in thick fur, which appear in late December or early January. By the end of the month these should start branching and by March the antlers, still covered in velvet, should be more or less fully grown, in a mature buck usually showing a full set of six points. Fraying will then take place and the new set of antlers will be cast around October/November. The antlers are usually about 8 inches long (20 cm) and seldom more than 10 inches (25 cm), with normally around six points, or tines, three on each side. In the young beast they are usually sharp and whitish. Thereafter the antlers should improve each year up to the age of six or seven as the buck matures. As the buck grows older the tines become blunter, the beams grow rougher and more rugged with vertical ridges or gutters, covered with crevices and channelling known as **gutters** and small growths known as **pearling**. The normal three points are termed the **brow, top** and **rear points**. The coronets will grow larger each year and the beams above them will thicken with more pearling.

As the buck grows older casting becomes steadily earlier and the antlers may be seen to be almost full grown and in velvet by the end of January. As he gets past his prime and starts going back the coronets tend to thicken and meet in the middle and the tines grow shorter and blunter with less pearling and thickness in the beams. Malformations sometimes occur when the antlers are damaged in velvet. A third beam, or irregular head with several points, may result. Damage to the testicles may result in the formation of what is known as a **perruque** head, when the antlers coalesce in a mass like a wig. Worst of all is the spike head with no tines, which of course is lethal and should be culled.

Description

Heights and weights
The species *Capreolus capreolus* is by far the smaller and more deli-

Roe. Young: Mature: Old

cate of the two indigenous British deer. The alert eyes and questing gaze, above the white patch of hair on the chin and front of the dark muzzle, give it an expression of curiosity, which is not entirely misleading. The roe deer tends to be curious by nature and sometimes this can be its undoing. With its dainty cloven hooves, cautious gait and delicate body it is an altogether enchanting deer to watch, whether feeding in woodland surroundings or in the open. When full grown the average buck and a mature doe are much the same size and again, as with any deer, much must depend on the nature and abundance of the available feeding. They will stand about 25 to 30 inches (63–76 cm) at the shoulder measuring about 44 inches (112 cm) from muzzle to rump and they will weigh between 45 and 65 pounds (20–29 kg). The less mature does will usually be slightly smaller, but this is usually more a matter of age than sex. There is no question, however, that the available feeding is the major deciding factor.

Colour and coat

The casting of the winter coat begins in April and continues into May or even later on occasions. In summer the coat is a bright reddish brown with a paler underbelly. In October it changes to a greyer colouring above with a more sandy effect below and although it has no tail the caudal disc beneath the rump develops the distinctive white colouring which flares conspicuously when retreating in alarm and is sometimes termed the **target**. European and Scandinavian roe are reputedly darker in colouring and in one or two areas in Britain, notably in Thetford Chase, where there have been introductions at one time or another, this is thought to be still apparent. Like most deer, however, roe do vary in colour in different areas and tend anyway to get darker with age. In some roe also a darker streak is visible down the back of the spine.

Age and teeth

How old a roe may live is difficult to say. Allowing for ordinary natural processes it is doubtful if they live much more than ten or twelve years and anything over fourteen must be exceptional. The young roebuck has a long slender neck and sloping rump. In middle age they have a well-filled-out body and neck and are obviously adult. The older roe have thicker bodies and carry the neck almost level with the body. In old age the head is held lower still and the gait is stiffer. To some extent the teeth can be used to assess age. By the fifteenth month the milk teeth have been replaced by adult teeth, which are at first very sharp. The grinding surfaces of the molars wear with age and by five years they will be almost smooth and beginning to show signs of wear. By ten to twelve years decay has started.

Gait and agility

Like the red deer, the roe has all the paces of a horse, but unlike the red deer it seldom trots from place to place, usually preferring to move in a gentle bounding canter. On being startled it may rush forward with its head down and then move off in a series of fast bounds before frequently stopping to look back to see what has alarmed it. On other occasions the roe will creep along in a hunched position through cover to avoid being noticed. They can jump extremely well and in full flight a six-foot (183 cm) fence is easily cleared, but in the normal course of events they prefer to go under obstacles such as fences. They can also swim well and have been observed crossing large stretches of water a mile or more across (2 km), although they tend to swim very low in the water with only their heads showing.

Slots and droppings

The slot is medium sized and the width of the heel is about 1½ inches (3.6 cm). The step is about 27 inches (68.5 cm) when walking normally. The fore and hind slots resemble each other. The dew claws are prominent in flight.

The droppings are usually single and a glossy dark brown or black colour, similar to but slightly larger than those of a hare or rabbit. They are frequently found near where lying up.

Powers of scent, eyesight, hearing and voice

Like all deer, the roe have remarkably fine scenting powers, and it is on this and their hearing that they mostly rely for their safety. Their eyesight, like that of the red deer, is not particularly good at picking out objects although they will distinguish movement very quickly. If curious as to the cause they will usually attempt to creep round so that they are downwind and can use their scenting powers to help them identify it. If alarmed they will bound off, frequently giving a loud bark at each bound. Although often taken to be alarm calls it quite frequently happens that while one of a group of roe is barking loudly others nearby are paying little or no attention.

The bark of the mature buck defending his territory is deep and challenging. The bark of a less mature buck is quite clearly different and when territory is being disputed no doubt this is immediately evident to both bucks concerned. The bark of an old doe is not always easily distinguishable from that of a buck. Some barks sound more like abuse than alarm. Indeed the barking of a roe roused by the approach of an intruder probably does not indicate fear so much as disturbance and very often, by the sound of it, irritation at being disturbed.

Habits

Relationships and social behaviour
The roebuck and doe are not strictly monogamous although they are frequently together. Small family groups of roe deer may be seen during the winter consisting of buck and doe, kids and yearlings, but these break up in the early spring with the approach of the rut. Unlike most deer it is extremely unusual for them to live in herds, although groups of as many as twenty or thirty may sometimes be seen feeding together in the winter. In the spring, however, as the small family groups break up, the young bucks begin to wander, sometimes several miles. A mature buck will drive off younger ones to find their own territory and in woodland will mark an area of about ten acres (4 ha) or thereabouts, or on higher ground as much as half a mile (1 km) in extent, as his home ground, by fraying trees with his antlers and by marking these chosen trees with the scent glands in his forehead between the antlers and at the inner corner of the eye. Territory may also be marked out by scent in the urine and scrapes will be seen on the ground acting as scenting markers.

The more a territory is challenged the greater the number of fraying stocks a buck will mark, and the size of these is a measure of the buck himself. He will at times also be heard barking a loud challenge as the rut approaches. In general roe tend to remain within their home territory for much of the year and in heavily stocked areas will probably not move much more than a mile or two (2–4 km) from it, although there are undoubtedly once or twice a year seasonal migrations, when all the roe in an area may move several miles. Various reasons have been suggested for this; a need to get onto higher ground away from flies; disturbance in ground; a need for change of pasturage and so on, but as they move by night and are seldom seen actually moving it is usually only possible to tell when these have taken place by the increased number on the ground. There is still room on many points about the roe for speculation and investigation.

Feeding

As with most deer their preferred feeding times are at dawn and dusk and through the night whenever conditions are suitable. They will eat a wide range of plants and herbage, but are finicky feeders choosing their food with care. They will consume bracken, fungi, heather, pine shoots, berries, grass, young leaves, flowers and even bushes such as privet, yew and elder which many animals will not touch.

Gestation, birth and growth of kids

Although the rut starts in July, much earlier than that of the red deer or other species, the kids are not born until the end of May, or early June, at much the same time as both red and fallow deer, although late fawns may be born up to August. This delayed gestation is one of the features which go to make the roe still such a fascinating mystery in many ways. The birth of twins is usual and triplets are known, but single kids may also be born. As with most deer, the birth is very quick. The kids are coloured a reddish brown with creamy spots down the flanks which they lose in late summer. Where twins are born they are usually taken to separate hiding places within a very short time. They are placed in cover in bracken, or similar beds, where they lie concealed like a hare in its form and remain silent unless disturbed, when they will screech loudly, making a considerable noise which will bring the doe running to their defence. During this period the kids are undoubtedly most at risk to foxes, or possibly even mink, but the rate of survival seems surprisingly high, suggesting that on the whole their camouflage is usually effective. After about three weeks the kids, like the red deer calves, are able to follow their mother and quickly learn to stay close to her white rump patch. The kids have a rather shrill and lamb-like call, which is answered with a more subdued piping sound from the doe, similar to her mating call.

In late May and June prior to the rut the doe often plays with the kids, chasing them for long periods in circles and figures of eight, leaping and jumping. These games may be both a preparation for the rut and also valuable training for the kids as well as exercising them. It makes a very attractive picture, although not something frequently observed as most does with kids at foot take care to spend much of their time in thick cover. Unless they come into the open or a clearing to feed they are not often seen. In August the does may leave their kids temporarily during the rut of the more mature does, which appears to follow that of the younger does. The kids, as they develop, follow their mother and the buck to whom she is attached and the small family group may be observed together until the following spring. The yearlings are then sent about their business as the doe prepares for another birth.

The rut
The rut takes place between July and August and although the does are gradually coming into season for some time they are only actually on heat for four days. The mating is a quick procedure, but the preliminaries for it may take days and there is a good deal still to be learned about it. The buck starts by showing attention to the doe and following her continuously, pressing her into a trot. Then the pace is likely to quicken. The doe will run in rings or figures of eight, with the buck following closely, frequently with his nose pressing on her posterior. The doe will sometimes make remarkable leaps and will frequently give a piping call to which the buck replies with grunting sounds. Quite often a series of rings are made. At the start of the rut these chases may be over a comparatively wide area, but as the heat develops they usually concentrate around one object, such as a tree, or bush, and although it has been suggested that the buck's object is to tire the doe so that she will stand for him, he is sometimes forced to halt and lie down panting. During this time the buck completely loses his normal caution and may often be seen during daylight hours.

There is also what is sometimes termed a false rut towards the end of October and the first part of November, when roe deer may again be seen chasing each other in a similar rutting performance. It is possible that this late stirring of the rut has some effect on the doe's fertilisation, for it has been established that the egg though fertilised does not in fact become implanted in the uterus until around December. It has been suggested that where for some reason a mating has not occurred previously it may now take place and this time there is no delayed gestation, so that it merely results in a birth in late June rather than early May. Does with newly born kids at foot, however, may sometimes be seen as late as early August, which would seem to indicate that this late rut may also have the usual delayed gestation.

Habitat

The roe is naturally a forest dweller and is at home in the woods. On the other hand, roe are very willing to adapt to circumstances and may be found in the open hill on the mountains of Scotland. They may also be found in downland, inhabiting rough patches, in Devon and in the Dorset and Hampshire vales. There is little doubt that with the cessation of the old shotgun drives and continuous persecution they have continued to spread over the past two decades into many areas where they have not previously been common.

Distribution

Roe deer are to be found throughout Scotland and most of northern England down to a line from about the Tees in the east to the Lune in the west. They are to be found in East Anglia and most of the southern counties and are steadily increasing their range. None, however, are to be found in Wales.

Part IV

Fallow Deer: *Dama dama*

Terminology

The male is known as a **buck**. The female is known as a **doe**. The young are known as **fawns**. Unlike either red or roe deer it is unknown for does to grow antlers.

Antler growth and terminology

The fallow buck sheds his antlers annually in April to May and they are usually free of velvet by September. Bucks without antlers are unknown. The antlers have brow, bay and tray tines, but are palmated, i.e., flattened towards the tips. The pedicles usually begin to develop in the fawn at about six to seven months, but at this stage are difficult to distinguish. At almost a year old, by the following May–June the antlers are well grown and are fully formed about mid-August when the velvet is shed. The first pair of antlers are simple spikes, hence the name pricket for the yearling buck. They are cast around June when the buck is two years old. When the ant-

lers are cast the bare root of the pedicle bleeds, but soon heals over.
In about three months the second head of antlers is free of velvet,
i.e. about the end of August.

The second pair of antlers may, or may not, be palmated, but the
size and shape of antlers varies greatly amongst individuals. Heads
are not generally considered to be in their prime until the eighth or
ninth head, i.e. by the time the buck is ten years of age. Abnormali-
ties arise, but anything such as perruque heads are much rarer than
amongst roebucks. Similarly although bucks without antlers, like
red deer, are known as hummels, this condition is also much rarer
amongst fallow bucks. A castrated buck kept in a park for fattening
is known as a **havier**.

Description

Heights and weights
The species *Dama dama* is probably the most familiar of the British
deer, mid-way in size between the red and the roe deer. The variations in colouring are such that it is hard to describe them, except
as typically cervine of medium size with all the attractive grace of
any deer in the wild. With their peculiarly bouncing gait it is understandable why they have so often been selected as suitable to grace
a parkland vista. There is little difference in size between bucks and
does, but when full grown the bucks will stand about 32 to 36
inches (81–96 cm) at the shoulder and the does about 32 to 34 inches
(81–86 cm) although, as always, much must depend on the available feeding. The average weight of the bucks is from 9 to 10 stone
(57–63 kg) and does from 7 to 8 stone (44–50 kg). A prominent
brush, or tail, about 6 inches (15 cm) long is a noticeable characteristic of fallow bucks.

The bucks and does have several barely visible scent glands,
interdigital, at the base of each leg above the cleaves, and intertar-
sal, just below the hock on the outside of the hind legs, also sub-
orbital, a gland just below the corner of each eye, which is filled
with a brown wax. The buck also has glands in the sheath of the
penis and the doe has glands around the vulva and anus which are
active during the oestrus.

Colour and coat
There are at least seven varieties of colour that may be encountered
in fallow deer in the wild, which explains why, when the antlers
are not in evidence, very often they are not immediately recognised

as fallow deer and may be mistaken for other species. The seven commonest varieties are:

Common fallow, which is a reddish brown, with white or beige spots in summer. In the winter it turns a darker brown on the upper part of the body with a pale grey on the lower part and loses its spots. The rump is light-coloured throughout the year. The fawns are spotted.

Menil is basically a paler version of the Common fallow. In the summer it is similar to the above but with more prominent spots. In winter the spots are still visible on a grey brown background. The fawns are spotted.

Black, as often seen in the New Forest. In the summer the upper part of the body is black and the lower part a sooty grey. In the winter the coat is duller, but remains much the same.

White, in summer are more of a creamy colour, but in winter turn more truly white. Fawns are without spots.

Blue, grey, or silver grey, are of a light roan colour, with blue-grey hairs over brown, or white with silver grey hairs giving a blue dun colouring. Fawns are not spotted.

Sooty-dun, in summer are liver coloured and in winter are so dark as to appear black.

Sandy, are a reddish brown with spots showing in both summer and winter. The fawns are spotted.

There are other colour variations, which explains why it is not always easy to identify a fallow deer without antlers.

Fallow deer moult twice a year, around April and at the end of September when the summer coat gives way to the woollier winter pelage. In the spring they often appear very moth-eaten and untidy during the moult.

Fallow doe galloping: kid leaping

Age and teeth

Fallow deer appear to live about twelve to fourteen years and any-thing much over sixteen in the wild is probably unusual, although they have been known to reach twenty in captivity. As a rough guide to telling the age by their teeth, by the 26th month the first teeth have been replaced and up to seven years the wear is pro-gressive until they are smooth. From about twelve to fourteen years decay has started.

Gait and agility

When alarmed the feral fallow is often indecisive. When first aware of danger they may take several stiff steps towards the source of alarm with their necks vertical and ears cupped forward, possibly stamping a forefoot. This rigid posture serves as an alarm signal. They will then bound away with the action peculiar to the fallow known as **pronking**, but they are likely to stop close to cover and look back to discover the source of their alarm. When they are much disturbed by dogs or shooting, however, they will depart at the first sign of danger at a fast and steady gallop. Their gaits are the walk, trot, a bounding canter and a full gallop. Like red deer they can jump extremely well and a six-foot fence is easily cleared. Like red deer they can swim extremely well and will sometimes shake them-selves like a dog on leaving the water.

Slots and droppings

The slot is medium-sized and the width at the heel about 2 inches (5 cm). The step is about 21 inches (52.5 cm) when walking normally. The fore and hind slots resemble each other. The marks of the dew claws are rarely evident.

The droppings are smaller than those of red deer and usually black and glossy when fresh. They are often in heaps, or strung out when the beast is moving.

Powers of scent, eyesight, hearing and voice

The fallow, like all deer, have very fine scenting powers and their hearing is also very good. In common with red and roe their eye-sight is good at detecting movement, but not so good at making out objects such as a stalker standing behind the cover of a bush. The doe will sometimes give a loud bark of alarm when frightened. When calling her fawn she gives a plaintive bleat and the fawn replies with a higher-pitched sound. The buck gives vent to a deep belching groan at intervals during the rut.

Habits

Relationships and social behaviour

Fallow deer are similar to red and sika deer in that they are gregarious and form herds. Like the red deer, however, the adult bucks form groups of bachelors for a good part of the year, living apart from the herds of does with yearlings and fawns. The two herds then combine together at the rut. Thus, like the red deer, the two herds of males and females are separate when the bucks are re-growing their antlers and the does are giving birth. Rather like the red deer, the older does tend to form a matriarchy and there appears to be a distinct peck order with regular precedence given to the senior doe, but the buck remains the dominant animal, even if, as is often the case, a doe leads the herd when they are disturbed. There appears to be no particular territorial instinct, except during the rut, and it is not clear how far fallow deer may at times roam. The probability is that with other herds in an area they may well travel considerable distances at times.

Feeding

Like most deer, fallow seem to be able to survive on a wide variety of sustenance, although obviously much depends on the area and what is available. They are predominantly grazers, but will browse contentedly on shrubs and trees. Feeding may include conifers, heather, holly, brambles, grasses, herbs, plants, fungi, acorns, beech mast, chestnuts, leaves, bark and, where available, frequently the contents of litter bins.

Gestation, birth and growth of kids

The rut takes place in late August and September and the gestation period is about seven and a half months. The fawns are thus usually born around mid-May onwards. Occasionally it seems late fawns may be born up to September, but this is clearly unusual. Fallow deer almost invariably only have a single fawn and twins are very rare. Fawns may be dropped anywhere, although usually away from the herd and in a place of some concealment. The doe is likely to lie down and the process has been observed to take about forty minutes, with the fawn standing and taking a few steps within twenty minutes. The fawn is well licked on birth and suckled within an hour or so. It is then hidden in a suitable bed and the doe seldom wanders more than two or three hundred yards away. It is fed about three times a day and the doe is prepared to attack any stray dogs or similar intruders, barking at them defiantly and striking out with the forefeet. The doe may give a bleating sound to which the fawn will respond with a shriller mewing sound. Like the red deer hind, the doe may paw a young fawn to make it remain concealed if it tries to follow her in the early stages. When danger approaches, as with other deer young, the fawn will freeze.

After a month or six weeks the fawn starts to follow its dam more frequently and by the time they are two months old fawns may be seen playing together and it is apparent that a group of fawns may be left gambolling together in the care of several adult does while their dams go off to feed elsewhere. As yearlings the young are separated from their mother when the rut commences again, but the bond between dam and doe is apparently often renewed afterwards and a doe may be seen followed by a fawn and a yearling doe.

The rut
In late August the bucks begin to migrate to the area where the doe herd is to be found. At the time of the rut the bucks exhibit territorial behaviour and defend their territories, or rutting **stands**. Like the roebuck, the fallow buck defines his rutting stand with scrapes made by pawing the ground and scraping with his antlers. He urinates a strong-smelling urine on these scrapes and uses his antlers to anoint himself with the mud. The buck will attack bushes and young trees, thrashing them repeatedly. He will also fray branches by rubbing his antlers on them. The former appears to be a form of release for aggression, while the latter appears to be a method of marking territory, as the suborbital glands close to the eyes are rubbed on the fraying posts and a distinct oily deposit is left. The sheath of the buck's penis turns inside out, turning black and rough and exuding a pungent smell, like a male goat. He starts to give voice at intervals with a deep belching groan.

Unlike the red deer he seldom has to herd the does, which gather round him freely at this time, although he may occasionally run after one that seems to be straying. He promenades around his territory chivvying the does and fawns. When groaning his tail curls up, he lifts his head horizontally and his suborbital glands open. When smelling the female he may raise his head and curl back his lower lip in the characteristic reaction known as the **flehmen**. Courtship may involve the buck chasing the doe prior to mating, but there is none of the prolonged chasing of the roe deer. Fights between bucks are usually decided largely by weight, since they will lock antlers and shove each other with all their power. There is a certain amount of clashing antler noise, but little real damage is likely to be caused. As long as they do not enter his territory the buck will not bother about other bucks around the scene and youngsters are also tolerated. It is only when another buck infringes his territory that a fight ensues. By mid-November the rut is over, the hinds have reverted to their herds; the bucks have also formed their separate herds, although the old bucks are usually on their own and hard to find.

Habitat
The fallow deer is normally a forest dweller, but will live also in the open if forced to do so. They prefer lowland woods with thick cover but may be seen on the outskirts in nearby fields at dusk. In quiet areas, however, they will feed and lie out in the open in daytime. The old bucks are almost entirely nocturnal and are seldom seen.

Distribution

Feral fallow are to be found in nearly every county in England. In Scotland they are to be found in nine counties, notably Perthshire, Inverness, Ross-shire, Sutherland and Caithness, Dumbartonshire, Morayshire, Argyll and Dumfriesshire. They are also present on three islands of the Scottish mainland, Islay, Mull and Scarba. There are a few in Wales.

Part V

Japanese Sika Deer: *Cervus nippon*

Terminology

As with red deer the male is known as a **stag** and the female as a **hind**. The young are known as **calves**.

Antler growth and terminology

The antlers are shed in the spring from April to May and are normally free of velvet by the end of August, or mid-September. The velvet, instead of being brown, is a greyish black. Male calves normally develop pedicles at about six months and usually form single unbranched spikes in the first year, varying in length from 1½ inches (4 cm) to as much as 10 inches (25 cm). In the third year the young stag develops six points, brow, tray and top. This is probably followed in a year or two by two more inward-pointing tines, making the normal full head of a mature stag of eight points with the bay points missing. Ten or even eleven points are sometimes encountered as a result of palmation of the main beam at the end.

Description

Heights and weights

It appears that several sub-species of sika may have been introduced to this country at various times and the sika deer in different areas vary considerably not only in size and appearance, but in habits and general behaviour. There is obviously a great deal more to be learned about them and they could repay further study. In general, however, the doe especially on first viewing may easily be mistaken for a fallow, or even a roe. The greyer head and large caudal patch outlined in black are, however, distinctive enough on closer acquaintance. The stag may stand 32 to 34 inches (81–86 cm) at the shoulder and the hind 30 to 32 inches (76–81 cm). The stag may weigh 8 to 10 stone (50–63 kg) and the hind about 6 to 7 stone (38–44 kg).

Colour and coat

The body colour is reddish brown with not very prominent yellowish spots on the flanks in the summer. In the winter the coat is darker brown above and greyish brown below. The head is generally paler and greyer than the body and there is a light-coloured U-shaped stripe above the eyes. At all times the caudal patch is very noticeably white, outlined in black. It flares when the deer is startled and is very prominent in flight. The metatarsal scent glands are light-coloured and very noticeable throughout the year. The calf is similar to a fallow fawn, but not as prominently spotted, with a light brown caudal disc.

Age and teeth

As with most feral deer it is difficult to estimate how old sika will live. Like roe, they will probably be considered old after nine or ten years and lucky if they survive much beyond twelve. Their age can be estimated by their teeth up to three years of age, by which time a full set of teeth including the third molar are present. After that it is a question of guesswork according to the amount of wear. The best that can be said is that it is adult, and after that old. Once decay has set in it may be termed very old.

Gait and agility
They have very similar gaits to the red deer, but the sika has a rather furtive way of moving at the walk. The stags move at a heavy gallop when alarmed.

Slots and droppings
The slot is medium-sized and the width at the heel is a little under 2 inches (5 cm) when walking normally. The fore cleaves are elongated unlike the hind cleaves which are shorter and more rounded. The dew claws are often visible.

The droppings are similar to those of the roe, but green and shiny if fresh and often found in heaps.

Powers of scent, eyesight, hearing and voice
Their powers of scent, eyesight and hearing are on a par with most deer and may be rated as generally acute. The stags have a peculiar whistling call, which, once heard, is quite unmistakable. It sounds very much as if someone was blowing a whistle. They will make several such whistles in quick succession then will be silent for a quarter or half an hour before repeating the performance. It can thus sometimes be quite difficult to locate them. At the height of the rut they are said to challenge each other with a sound described as like 'blowing a raspberry'. Their alarm signal is a squeal, but in the main they are notably silent and secretive. The hind has a plaintive bleat which is attractive to the stag and the calf makes a peeping sound like a fallow fawn.

Habits

Relationships and social behaviour
The behaviour of the sika apparently varies considerably in different areas and in some places the stags are territorial during the rut, whereas in others their behaviour is similar to that of red and fallow in that they form harems of hinds. They are certainly gregarious to a certain extent and form herds, but generally on a smaller and looser scale than red or fallow deer. The stags have been known to hybridise with red, but this has not been known to occur with the hinds. Stags are known to associate with hinds outside the rutting season, but for much of the year the hinds and calves at foot

appear to associate in small loosely-knit groups of from three up to
twelve. The males tend to form larger groups of from ten to twenty.

Hind calves remain with the mother until she is due to calve
again when they are driven off and the split then appears to be permanent, as yearlings are not usually seen with a hind and calf. The
stag calves are gathered together by the adult stags from January to
about March and taken off to join the stag herds. Solitary stags are
also met with as often as small groups. In different parts of the
country it is apparent their behaviour differs considerably, but that
of the stags is generally more secretive and by no means fully understood as yet.

Feeding
The evidence from some areas suggests the sika is mainly a grazer,
whereas in others it appears to be quite a frequent browser. There is
evidence that they may feed mainly on grass and herbage, but are
notably fond of hazel shoots and will strip the bark from medium-
thick branches. They also apparently in some areas like feeding in
estuarian belts on sea couch-grass during the spring and early
summer. Although it seems they may be predominantly grazers
they will certainly browse in plantations and will also eat fruits,
fungi and similar feeding when available. The probability is that, as
with most deer, much depends on their location and circumstances.

Gestation, birth and growth of calves
As with fallow deer, gestation is about seven and a half months.
The general treatment of the calves is similar to fallow deer. The
growth is very rapid and a hind calf will be full-grown at two years
old, although a male calf will take longer to reach full maturity.

The rut
As with red deer, the rut takes place towards the end of September
but extends on through October until the end of November. In
some areas the master stags are known to mark out a territory of
around 20–30 acres (8–12 hectares). In this it seems they may establish a platform, or rutting stand. Although the master stag will tol-
erate the presence of other stags in his territory they will also fight
fiercely for the possession of the hinds. In other areas they will conduct a harem of hinds in much the same way as a red stag. A special
feature of the sika stag in rut that has been noted is that they sometimes produce thick milky fluid from the suborbital glands. As

already noted, the stags have a peculiar whistling call, which develops into something like a roar in the rut.

Habitat
They prefer woodland and are mainly nocturnal in their habits, but may be seen at dawn and dusk feeding in the open. Where not unduly disturbed they may also quite often be seen out in the open during the day.

Distribution

Feral sika have been seen in Devon, Dorset, Hampshire, Kent, Lancashire, Oxfordshire, Somerset, Surrey, Sussex, Wiltshire and Yorkshire. In Scotland they are found in Angus, Argyll, Caithness, Fife, Inverness, Peebles, Ross and Sutherland.

Muntjac: Chinese or Reeves's muntjac: *Muntiacus reevesi* and Indian Muntjac: *Muntiacus muntjak*

Terminology

The male is known as a **buck** and the female as a **doe**: the young are termed **fawns**.

Antler growth and terminology

Pedicles are evident in the young male from five months and grow for a further three to four months, but whether they will develop into antlers depends on the time of year as the antlers only grow from May to September. Therefore, if born in January, a young male should have achieved his first button antlers by September. If born later they may remain in velvet until the following September. The velvet is noticeably dark in colour. As the antlers develop with age they appear to grow a more pronounced backwards curve. The length is about 2½ to 3 inches (6–7.5 cm) and consists of one short brow tine and an unbranched beam. The antlers grow from long skin-covered pedicles which extend down the forehead giving the deer the name **rib face**. The bucks have small tusks nearly an inch and a half (4 cm) long.

Description

Heights and weights

They are noticeably short in the leg and their bodies tend to have a rather hunched appearance, but the ribbed face is possibly their most notable feature and with their blunt muzzles gives a rather Roman-nosed effect to the head. There are probably two species and possibly hybrids in the wild, as follows:

At the shoulder the buck measures: Indian: 22–23 inches (56–58.5 cm); Reeves's: 17–18 inches (43–46 cm); Hybrid: 19–20 inches (48–51 cm). The doe in each case measures about three inches (7.5 cm) less. The average weight of the buck is Indian: 30 lbs (13 kg); Reeves's: 25 lbs (11 kg); Hybrid: 26–28 lbs (11.5–12.5 kg). The doe is generally two to five pounds (1–2 kg) lighter.

Colour and coat

Indian: deep chestnut body, dark back, paler underneath. Reeves's a redder chestnut. When running off, the tail, in both buck and doe about six inches (15 cm) long, is raised showing a white underside.

Age and teeth

They are known to live to nine or ten, when they may be considered to be going back and anything over that may be considered old, with a possible life-span of twelve to fourteen years at most. Both male and female have canine teeth, reaching a length in the male of about 1½ inches (4 cm). The adult canine tooth is present at five months. In mature males they become broken and by nine years may be worn down to the gum.

Gait and agility

Their usual method of moving from place to place is a steady trot, but when alarmed they can move extremely fast and usually make for the nearest cover, where they quickly vanish from sight. Their habit of holding their heads low when moving fast, which no doubt greatly assists them following runs in cover, combined with their hunched appearance, looks somewhat unattractive, but does not detract from their speed. They are capable of jumping five feet (152 cm) easily.

Slots and droppings

The slot is only about ¾ inch (2 cm) wide at the heel. Quite frequently the inner cleave is slightly smaller and more pointed than the outer one. The length of a step is about 8 inches (21 cm) at a normal walk. The dew claws do not usually show, except in deep mud.

The droppings are shiny, smooth and almost black. The does tend to make a heap in one place and others may add to them.

Voice
Muntjac are known as 'the barking deer'. They will give a single bark at about five second intervals for up to three-quarters of an hour or more. Sometimes two or three will bark together. The fawns squeak at similar intervals if lost. The does squeak when sexually aroused and the male will sometimes grunt.

Habits

Relationships and social behaviour
The family group appears generally to consist of the buck and doe, half-grown youngster and fawn. Fawns are dropped at about seven-month intervals, whereupon copulation follows within three days. The fawn will remain with the mother until after the birth of the next fawn. It then appears it is driven away by degrees by the aggressive behaviour of the parents and it is thought that conception is possible from about six months onwards. There is obviously still a lot to be learned about this species, as with sika and roe.

Feeding
They are grazers and browsers with catholic tastes, covering the whole gamut of deer feeding. They will normally feed for about twenty minutes to half an hour and then ruminate. It has been noted that they find it difficult to survive a hard winter, as their short legs make it difficult for them in deep snow, and they are apparently hard put to it to find feeding and shelter.

The rut
There is no set season for the rut and the fawns may be born at any time, but normally only one. Twins are rare.

Distribution

They are to be found chiefly in a large diamond with the apex around Sheffield, the sides on the Norfolk coast and Welsh border and the base above Southampton. They appear to be increasing in numbers and colonising fresh areas very quickly. Whether they will continue to do so after a series of hard winters remains to be seen.

Chinese Water Deer: *Hydropotes inermis*

Terminology

The male is known as a **buck** and the female as a **doe**. The young are known as **fawns**. Not a great deal appears to be known about the species and it would clearly repay further study.

Description

Heights and weights
They stand slightly higher behind, but are graceful-looking deer, although without antlers. The buck has prominent tusks about 2⅜ inches (5.5 cm) long, protruding well below the jawline, which can inflict a nasty wound. The does have very short upper canines. They are a reddish brown in summer, greyer in the winter. They have a tail 3 inches (7.5 cm) long, but it is rarely visible and there is no trace of white to be seen in the tail region. The bucks stand about 20 inches (51 cm) at the shoulder and weighs 25–30 lbs (11–13.5 kg). The doe stands 19–20 inches (48–51 cm) and weighs 20–25 lbs (9–11 kg).

The rut
Territories are marked with scrapes. The rut takes place mainly in December when the bucks may fight with a clicking of tusks.

Gestation and growth of fawns
The gestation period is about 180 days and the fawns are mostly born in June or July. Twins and triplets are common and more have been recorded. They are weaned in two months and sexually mature in six.

Gait and agility
They are fast movers and can jump well, but have a habit of squatting down in the open after running a short distance.

Voice
The alarm cry is a harsh repeated bark. They will bark repeatedly to each other, or at an intruder, including humans. The doe makes squeaking sounds when sexually aroused.

Distribution

Chiefly established in Bedfordshire, Buckinghamshire, Hampshire and Shropshire, into East Anglia.

4

Preliminary Considerations and Equipment

The initial choices

The sheer diversity of the ground over which stalking may take place and the variety of deer which may be encountered are the first and possibly greatest problems facing any would-be stalker, since they may be radically different in every part of the country. In the highlands, for example, a deer forest may consist of over 100,000 acres (40,485 ha) of bare mountainside, with seemingly no sign of trees, or indeed feeding for anything barring possibly a goat. Yet here, in secluded corries or hollows, in this outwardly inhospitable landscape there will often be found surprisingly lush pastures hidden away. In other parts, patches of heather, or small copses of windswept trees will provide not only feeding but shelter for the red deer which are to be found there in surprising numbers. The occasional roe deer may also be found in this type of ground which have adapted to life in these barren uplands with surprising ability, stunted though their antlers and growth may be compared with others in lusher lowland ground.

Yet not all highland deer forests are necessarily so barren, or so extensive, for there are some which comprise no more than 8,000 acres (3,238 ha) where as many as fifty stags may be shot annually. Others have surprisingly large areas of afforested land. In yet others sika and fallow deer may be encountered as well as red and roe. Thus each deer forest has its distinct characteristics and even its differing heads and types of deer. One may be known as principally a stag forest, whereas another nearby is mainly a hind forest. Such variation is inevitable with the diversity of ground and the habits of the deer themselves.

In the lower ground the possible differences between areas quite close together are even greater and more marked, for here the amazing diversity of the British countryside makes for even more variety. In one part, as in Cumbria and the Lake District, there may be rolling upland, in another the wooded and chequer-board pattern of the English shires. Further south may be found the flat lands of East Anglia, interspersed with breckland and forest as in Thet-

71

ford Chase. So one may progress past Epping Forest across London to the sandy heathlands of Surrey and along the south coast to the New Forest and the Hampshire downs, over Wiltshire and Dorset to the deep combes of Devon.

All these varied landscapes have their equally varied populations of deer, from red, roe and fallow in Cumbria and in Thetford Chase further south. The roe, the red, sika and fallow may be found in the New Forest and roe and red deer with some fallow in Devon. New-comers such as the muntjac and the Chinese water deer are liable to be encountered in an ever expanding area around Woburn. With each county's changing landscape the deer are likely to vary with the background. This makes for the essential variety of stalking, but it also poses an initial problem for the would-be stalker. In each county, in neighbouring vales, the sport may be entirely different. While 8,000 acres (3,238 ha) might be a small highland deer forest, some 2–3,000 acres (809–1,219 ha) may be a large area elsewhere. The problem for the novice faced with such a bewildering choice is simply knowing where to start.

Gaining the initial experience

Unless the would-be stalker has friends who own a deer forest in Scotland, or who have roe, fallow, red, sika, or other stalking avail-able in low ground in Scotland or England, there is the initial prob-lem of gaining experience. Undoubtedly one of the best ways of learning initially is to approach the Deer Society of Great Britain, which arranges annual stalkers' courses. These will provide the novice with all the necessary background knowledge he is likely to require. At the same time those attending them will gain some valu-able hints as to where to go for stalking. As well as disseminating knowledge about deer, encouragement of potential deer-stalkers is, after all, one of the prime aims of the Society.

If it is not possible to attend one of these courses then probably the most obvious way to gain initial experience may be to approach the Forestry Commission, who let some casual stalking under supervision, or else to scan the advertisments in sporting journals such as *The Shooting Times, The Field, Country Life, Country Sport, The Sporting Gun, Shooting News* or *The Scottish Field*, and follow up any hotel, or sporting agency, advertising stalking as available with professional stalkers. There are many of these and some of them provide very good sport indeed along with tuition for beginners. In such cases arrangements will be made to provide rifle, ammunition, and a temporary Firearms Certificate as well as insurance cover. The costs will vary depending on what is required, but inevitably it is not likely to be cheap.

As a less expensive alternative, to gain initial experience and a foretaste of the sport, it may be that the would-be stalker has comparatively easy access to a large park such as Richmond, Windsor Great Park, or better still some large areas of common land, such as Epping Forest, or the New Forest, or one of the National Parks, where deer of various kinds are known to be plentiful. Then, with a pair of binoculars it is possible to start studying deer at first-hand in their natural habitat. Using the wind correctly it should be possible to learn quite a lot just by seeing how close to deer in such conditions it is possible to stalk.

In many of the National Parks, or areas such as the New Forest, the average casual visitor might well be unaware that deer are even present were it not for the warning signs by the roadsides. They are there in numbers that may surprise even the knowledgeable, but to find them will probably entail early morning, or dusk, vigils, which may, or may not, prove successful. There is no doubt, however, that stalking, with binoculars and possibly with a camera as well, in this way can not only prove very satisfying, but also an extremely good preparation for the real thing. An essential preliminary, however, is to check with the authorities, if only in the shape of a keeper, or ranger, as to whether there is any danger of being in the way of legitimate stalkers, also as to where you may and may not go and the best and most likely places to find deer. The likelihood is that you will receive every help possible, not least because such requests seriously made are a pleasant change from the usual run-of-the-mill queries. At the very least this sort of approach to deer stalking should provide useful experience.

Physical and mental preparedness

In almost any form of stalking it is desirable to be fit, since at the very least in low ground stalking it may involve hauling considerable weights in the shape of dead deer for some distances, and on the hill, in the Scottish highlands, it may involve walking for as much as twenty miles (32 km) over rough terrain. It is also desirable to become acclimatised to remaining still for long periods despite the attentions of flies and midges in summer or icy conditions and sleety rain in winter. It is also essential to be prepared to get soaking wet, crawling on your hands and knees, or even on your belly, up

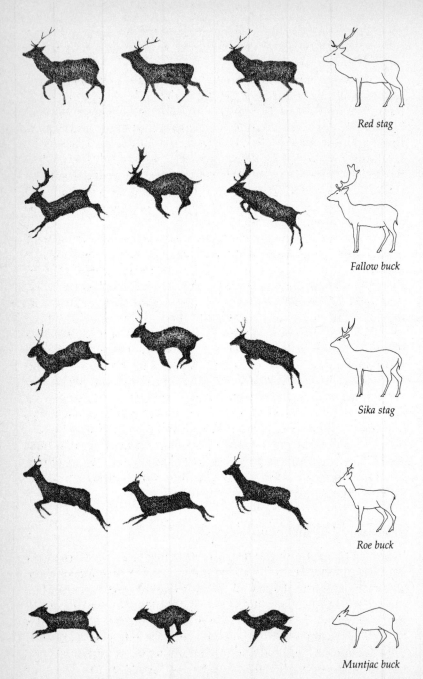

Red stag

Fallow buck

Sika stag

Roe buck

Muntjac buck

Comparative gaits

narrow forestry ditches or across muddy bogs.

At the end of a day which might well be regarded as suitable for an infantry army training course, there may be nothing to show for it whatever and the rifle may not even have been fired. On the other hand, a heavy beast may have been grassed far from the nearest track suitable for vehicles, or beyond the reach of the pony; then a lengthy haul after an exhausting day may still be necessary, although the satisfaction inherent in having fulfilled the object of the exercise will probably make it all seem worthwhile. If you can face up to all, or any, of these prospects, certain that you can survive without breaking down under the strain, then you are at least starting on the right lines. If you are prepared to gralloch your own beast, haul or carry it to a point where it can be hoisted into a vehicle and attend to it on your return, hanging it up and finally skinning and buttering it yourself, then you are undoubtedly starting on the right lines.

The attitude of mind

Of course, deer stalking does not need to be such an energetic pastime. Just as the Edwardian stalkers went up the hill on the back of a pony, so now it is possible to go up the hill to a suitable easy starting point in a tracked, or wheeled, vehicle suited to the job, or even by helicopter. As in the Edwardian days it may then only be a question of following the stalker to a suitable position overlooking the deer, being handed the loaded rifle, taking the shot and either killing, or missing, the stag, then returning home after watching the beast being gralloched and taking a photograph to commemorate the event.

On the low ground it is possible to take a landrover to the foot of a platform, or high seat, in the early evening. From this point of vantage it may then only be a question of waiting patiently for a matter of half an hour before a suitable beast presents itself within range. Then, again, it may be only a question of taking a shot and killing, or missing. The actual gralloch and hauling of the buck, or stag, onto the landrover may again be left to the professional stalker. Once again a photograph may be taken to commemorate the event. If this is all you require from your sport, if trophy heads are all you are interested in, like our Edwardian forebears, then it is merely a matter of paying for it.

Like so much else in life, however, the enjoyment obtained from a sport is more often measured in the amount of effort you put into it rather than the amount of money expended. The knowledge of having extended every effort to outwit a beast of the wild in its natural habitat and having succeeded in doing so is often enough. The shot itself, as any stalker worth knowing will agree, is almost the least important part of the proceedings, except that it should be performed properly, so that the beast dies instantly.

Since man has upset the natural ecology of the wild it is important that the balance is maintained artificially. The culling of deer in correct proportions according to the numbers on the ground is a part of this controlling procedure. That it is regarded as a sport, that deer antlers are regarded as trophies for their size or shape, is by the way. The serious stalker should not consider the size or shape of a head as of prime importance. He should think of the beast as the one that is best removed for the general improvement of the remainder, or for the betterment of the surroundings.

Thus, for instance, a young roebuck may have a poor head compared with a nearby older buck, but it may well be preferable from the point of view of the growing trees to cull the lesser beast rather than remove the finer head and cause inferior bucks to damage the growing timber in their efforts to establish territories, where the older buck had reigned undisputed. A red stag may be a hummel without antlers, or a switch with murderous antlers, capable of killing better deer in the rut, and both are always better out of the way and should be shot in preference to far better heads should the opportunity ever arise. Unless the beginner is prepared to consider points such as these and abide by them he would do better not to stalk at all. The ability to make such decisions is only acquired by knowing the ground and by experience, but the would-be stalker should understand the necessity for them before he starts.

Time required

A great advantage of deer stalking is that in one form or another it is available throughout the year. The would-be stalker, however, must decide beforehand how much time he can afford to give his sport. If it is possible to spare only a week or a fortnight each year then it is a question of deciding what is available and most desired at that time. It may be a choice of taking a rifle in a deer forest in the highlands and shooting a number of stags, or else, if that is too expensive, it may be possible to take a fortnight assisting the professional cull of the hinds. This is no easy task at a time of year when the weather is likely to be bitterly cold on the mountains, but it is a necessary one and still requires considerable skill and effort. Stalking the old hinds can indeed often be a much more difficult task than stalking the stags earlier in the year, especially when the approaching rut has made them less wary than usual.

Alternatively, low ground shooting, at roe, fallow, red or sika, or even muntjac and Chinese water deer, may be more readily available and may seem more appealing. Stalking in woodland or shooting from a stand, or a high seat, is generally a less arduous pursuit than stalking on the hill, but it requires a high degree of concentration and skill. It can also be a strenuous enough business in certain conditions, especially when it is necessary to haul a heavy beast any great distance. It may be that a professional stalker is available to act as a guide and adviser, but quite often after a certain amount of experience has been gained it is possible to come to some arrangement with a landowner to take an area of suitable ground on mutually agreed terms, depending to a certain extent on what is shot.

If the would-be stalker wishes to spend all his available spare time stalking, rather than merely devoting his annual holiday to the sport, this is, of course, quite another matter. From a purely geographical viewpoint the odds are inevitably much greater that the would-be stalker lives closer to low ground stalking of one sort or another than to stalking in the highlands. In general it is also more likely that a would-be stalker could afford to spend time each week on low ground near to his home if necessary, even if this was only on Saturday and Sunday mornings. The ability to spend many hours on the ground is almost an essential for the serious low ground stalker. Owing largely to human interference in their habitat, deer are mainly to be seen on low ground or afforested areas at dawn and dusk. In this TV age few people nowadays are to be seen stirring in the countryside at dawn, when the stalker must be abroad. On the other hand, to rise at 3.30 or 4.00 in the morning and finish stalking by 8.00 is not conducive to doing a full day's work thereafter. Some people have been known to manage it successfully, but others as a direct result have been known to fall asleep in the middle of board meetings or similarly inauspicious occasions. Each individual must make his own decisions about how much time he can spare for his sport and act accordingly.

Knowledge of the ground

It is essential in any form of stalking for the stalker to know his ground. In the first place, it is important to learn the boundaries on the map and to get to know them before starting to explore the ground in the centre. Depending on the area involved this is likely to take some time in itself. The average highland stalker probably learns his ground from an older man who knows it well already and can point out all the important landmarks and the important deer passes, the usual effects of wind and weather in each area and the expected reactions of the deer. It is more often than not likely to be a season or two before even an experienced new man has begun to settle down in any large stretch of highland forest. To a lesser degree the same thing applies to most low ground stalking. To know the boundaries is the first important point and after that to find out the general movements of the deer within those boundaries is the next task. How the wind and the weather affect the movements of the deer and the best points of observation in various conditions are also important factors to learn. Dependent on the size of the area, it is again likely to take even an experienced stalker a season or more before he begins to feel confident of his knowledge of the ground in all conditions.

It is thus apparent that the person who wishes to spend most of the year stalking has to be able to adapt his life so that he can put in some unusual hours. The full-time low ground stalker or keeper may be out at dawn and dusk almost every day for months on end, more or less regardless of the weather. The keen amateur can afford to indulge himself occasionally, when he has begun to know his ground and the deer on it. A moonless night with a steady breeze in the evening will probably mean perfect stalking conditions in the morning, with the deer feeding late, having been unable to see enough to feed during the night. A moonlit night and a wet dawn may mean the deer are probably in cover after feeding all night and hence a wasted journey. As he grows more experienced the deer stalker knows almost certainly where his deer will be. It is the same on the hill. After a steady gale from one direction the hill stalker knows without looking that most of his deer will be in well-protected areas in various parts of his ground. Such knowledge is an instinctive result of experience on the ground and can only be acquired over a number of years. It is necessary, however, to put first things first. Before attaining such heights of experience, indeed before starting to learn to stalk, first of all it is desirable to obtain a suitable rifle, and to buy that it is essential to obtain a

Firearms Certificate. If the applicant is of good character the procedure is not unduly complicated.

The Firearms Certificate (and Game Licence)

Before buying a rifle an application must be made at the local police
station for a Firearms Certificate, which is signed by the Chief Constable after due enquiry as to where the applicant proposes to use
it, his character and antecedents. Thus, immediately, a chicken and
egg situation arises which may easily deter the novice at the start so
that the wish to stalk dies stillborn before the would-be stalker has
even reached the stage of deciding what sort of rifle is required.
Theoretically, of course, anyone who lends his rifle to another to
use is committing an offence under the conditions on which a
Firearms Certificate is issued. In practice, there must undoubtedly
be a great many who break this law either deliberately or inno-
cently. There is no doubt that in this case the Law, in the shape of
the police, can often appear somewhat obstructive, but with the
many armed robberies being committed this is perhaps not
altogether surprising.

As has been indicated, a temporary Firearms Certificate valid for
a fortnight can be obtained for a visitor to the country, or a hotel
guest, with a full month's warning beforehand, but this can
generally be left to the hotel or estate agent to arrange. When applying for a Firearms Certificate, however, it is necessary to say where
the rifle will be used and this will mean having written permission
from a landowner to use the rifle on his ground for the specific purpose of shooting deer and, as a matter of normal procedure, the
police will, of course, check the facts with him. Should you wish to
change the ground over which you shoot this will necessitate a
further application to the police.

In addition, the Firearms Certificate will include details of all ammunition bought and also any changes of firearm. Each change in a
Certificate costs £20, so this should mentally be added on to the cost
of the rifle when contemplating changing, or adding to those
already owned. It should also, perhaps, be noted that if it is desired
to use rifled slugs in a shotgun a Firearms Certificate is required
before they can be bought. Before actually shooting any deer it
should also be remembered that you are required by law to have a
Game Licence, which can be obtained from any Post Office.

The rifle

It is illegal to shoot deer with a rifle of a calibre less than .240 or a
muzzle energy of less than 1700 foot pounds. It must also fire a soft-
nosed, or hollow-nosed, bullet. The basic question is, what type of
deer are likely to be the main quarry? For shooting roe deer a .243 is
perfectly adequate. In the past a .22 hornet, or .222 was considered
sufficient, although now no longer legally permitted. The fact of the
matter is, of course, that any bullet put in the right place will kill,
but it is the certainty of placing it correctly that is the problem. Too
light a bullet in the wrong place may maim or wound a beast, causing it to die painfully later, food only for foxes and crows. Hence
these legal limitations.

There are those who advocate heavy rifles and powerful ammunition, but it is difficult to improve on the advice of Mr W. D. M.
Bell, M.C., the celebrated elephant hunter in Africa between the
two world wars, who used to use a .256 on all big game including
elephants, but added the advice: 'keep perfectly cool and . . . never
. . . hurry . . . never fire unless you can see your way to place a
bullet in a vital spot . . . (then) the calibre of the bullet makes no difference.'

The modern high-velocity rifle fires a virtually flat trajectory,
while that used by Mr Bell had a curving trajectory. Today, the .243
will kill red deer perfectly adequately, although there are those
who may claim that it is desirable to use a .270. Although all their
employees do not necessarily follow their lead, the Forestry Commission issues .270 rifles as standard for use on all deer by their
employees. The argument against the heavier rifle and ammunition
is simply that the recoil is slightly greater and the rifle must therefore be held more firmly, which sometimes makes for stiffness in
use and may cause flinching. This in turn, of course, can lead to
missing. The larger the bullet, also, naturally enough, the more
damage to the carcase of the deer and when missed the greater the
danger to others. The safety margin is therefore one to consider,
especially in areas where there are houses, or roads on which
people might be passing within reasonable proximity. Safety is of
paramount importance whenever handling a rifle.

It would be invidious to mention any one make as preferable to
another. Either of these calibres is available from makers such as
Parker Hale or B.S.A. in the U.K., or Winchester, Martin, Reming-
ton, Ruger, or Savage from the U.S.A., or Browning from Belgium,
Mannlicher from Austria, Mauser from Germany, Brno from Cze-

choslovakia, Sako and Tikka from Finland and many others.

As regards ammunition, the standard loads for the .270 are 100, 130 and 150 grains. For the technically minded, the 130 has a muzzle velocity of some 3,140 feet per second. At 200 yards the trajectory only rises 2 inches (5 cm) with an energy of around 2,000 foot pounds. It is difficult to improve on that performance. On the other hand, the standard ammunition for the .243 is just about as good with both 80 and 100 grain. The 80 grain has a muzzle velocity of about 3,500 feet per second and a muzzle energy of about 2,200 foot pounds. Its trajectory rises less than 2 inches (5 cm) at 200 yards. It is difficult to wish for any better results than these. If you wish to go into hand-loading, or feel you can improve on these, that is up to you.

Whatever rifle is chosen it is desirable that it should fit and it is worth having it fitted properly. Nor is it desirable to choose too light a rifle on the grounds that it will be carried all day. If it is too light it is likely to have a heavier recoil, which can be a much more tiresome factor. Nor, for the same reason, is it desirable to have too short a barrel, although at first sight it would seem there are advantages in carrying a short-barrelled gun through thick cover since it does not get so easily caught in twigs and branches. This is true enough, but again if the recoil is greater the advantages on the one hand are lost on the other.

In Continental rifles particularly, many are fitted with an alternative hair trigger mechanism, either by using two triggers or by pushing the single trigger forward. Personally, I do not see any advantage in these arrangements and dislike hair triggers intensely. In my view the normal arrangement of a single trigger with light first pressure and six or eight pound second pressure is very hard to beat.

The sling
A sling for the rifle is essential, not only for easier carriage, but also for the undoubted advantage it provides, if properly used, in steadying aim and making for better shooting. The sling should fit directly onto the rifle swivels and should not have metal clips, as these can be noisy. The best type of sling is of broad leather which will not readily slip or bite into the shoulder as a narrow one will. Braided leather is good but picks up dirt easily. It should have an adjustable strap so that it can be fitted to the individual using it. It should fit comfortably, so that the arm can be slipped easily inside it and instant support be provided for the shot. It should be kept well

oiled and supple. As an integral part of the rifle and the shooting process its importance cannot be overstressed.

Rifle cleaning equipment

It is essential to keep your rifle in good order and it should always be cleaned after being taken out, whether it has been fired or not. A suitable metal cleaning rod is not expensive. A supply of flannel patches to fit on the jag, or a roll of tow, for cleaning, combined with a suitable oil is all that is required. After any outing, however, the rifle should be stripped down as a matter of course to be cleaned and oiled, for it is only too easy to pick up mud, or dirt, even on an outing when nothing has been seen and it has never been used. A strip of sellotape across the muzzle will help, but it is important to remember to remove it before use.

The telescopic sight

As late as the 1960s telescopic sights were often regarded as somewhat unnecessary appendages and at least one leading authority on deer stalking claimed that the open sight was better. The fact of the matter is, however, that they are an improvement on the human eye. Whatever type is used they allow for shooting when light is fading and the foresight of an open sight would be almost invisible. The only time when they are inferior to open sights is in driving rain, when they are virtually useless, although with transparent covers they can be used very briefly for one quick shot. They are undoubtedly desirable in that they can generally assure a kill with more certainty than without one. The aim is always to ensure the cleanest kill with the least possible margin of error, therefore they are to be thoroughly commended.

Having said that, it must be remembered that they do not in themselves guarantee success. They are only as efficient as the man behind them. At all times a rifle has to be held straight on target to achieve results. Shutting the eyes, or flinching, with or without a telescopic sight, will as surely result in a miss. Jerking on the trigger instead of squeezing gently with the breath held will also result in a miss. The telescopic sight is not a cure-all for every fault. It is merely an aid to better shooting.

The type of sight used is up to every individual, but in my view it is better to buy the best telescopic sight and a cheaper rifle than the other way round. Those with the most light-receptive qualities and largest diameter with bloomed lenses are the best. The modern telescopic sights can be either fixed, or variable. The variable has the obvious advantage that you can set it at the same magnification as a fixed 'scope, or increase the magnification if you wish. The only objection I can see to them is that they may encourage some people to take shots at too great a range.

Switch in the sights

There are, of course, various types of graticule available, starting with fine cross-hairs, which it is claimed may get lost as darkness is gathering and light is fading when seen against a dark-skinned quarry. The post and rails, or upright post with a fine cross hair are alternatives which many prefer. Others are the post and rails with an inverted hair-line graticule making a cross in the centre, or the post and rails with an inverted post and cross hairs in the centre. It is largely up to the individual to make his own choice and accustom himself to it.

One advantage of the cross graticules with measurements on them on a fixed sight is that it is possible to estimate the range by seeing how many graticules the deer takes on the cross hairs. This can be very useful on occasions. For instance when firing across a valley you may be further than you thought. It very often happens that when measuring range downhill, or across a gap, one underestimates through lack of any of the normal markers to aid distance measurement. In such circumstances the graticules can be of very great assistance.

It is also extremely important to make sure that the telescopic sight is correctly fitted. If it is too close to the eye when taking aim the recoil can give you a very nasty cut around the eyebrow. It should be fitted so that there is sufficient clearance between the eye and the eyepiece when taking a sight. This is a point which is often overlooked until the damage has been done and there are many experienced stalkers who share a scar of this type. Be warned and have a care.

The sight aligner

As an aid to sighting-in the telescopic sight it is well worth investing in a telescopic sight aligner. With steel rods to fit most calibres and a marked grid on which the telescopic sight can be adjusted, they are a simple means of setting the sights accurately. Although initially expensive, these sight aligners are likely to save considerable expenditure over the years on ammunition wasted by sighting-in the telescopic sights. They are also useful in checking the sights whenever it is feared they may have been knocked out of alignment, or just to instil confidence by ensuring the sights are correct at the start of the day.

The rifle sleeve

For the hill at least, it is absolutely essential to have a sleeve for the rifle with a sling attached. It is as essential that this is large enough for the rifle, with telescopic sight attached, to be easily removed from it with the minimum of noise. The old canvas sleeve with a base opening strap is still in use and can be quite effective in dry weather. They do have a tendency to stick a bit, however, and a heavy-duty zip on a wool- or rubber-lined sleeve is probably a considerable improvement. Waterproof P.V.C. is a considerable improvement on either leather or canvas, for the latter can more easily get sodden in very wet conditions. The advantage of a full-length zip and woollen or rubber lining is that, after use, it can be completely unzipped and dried out, whereas those rifle sleeves which only open at one end are much more difficult to dry out thoroughly. The woollen, or rubber, lining, although adding slightly to the weight, also provides a useful added protection against the almost inevitable knocks.

The ammunition container

Nowadays most ammunition is sold in convenient polystyrene containers which hold the individual rounds without their rattling about. Even so these are easily enough damaged and it is worthwhile having a leather ammunition holder with loops for individual rounds which slips into the pocket. It is possible to buy belts and bandoliers, but then the ammunition is not protected and it savours a little too much of the wild west. A wallet that fits in the pocket and holds a minimum of ten rounds, preferably twenty, is much more convenient. It is also a good plan to have separate wallets for each type of ammunition, so that there is then no danger of making the mistake of going out with the wrong type of ammunition for the rifle, which can be easily done and may ruin the day.

Binoculars

These are another item of stalking equipment where it pays to buy the best you can afford. Nowadays there are very powerful binoculars available with central focusing and zoom lenses, which at a touch provide close-up vision. You may, however, prefer binoculars with individual adjusting lenses and that is up to the individual. Whatever type of binoculars are used they should combine lightness and toughness. They should not have metal pieces which may clink against buttons, or other objects. If they do they should be bound with sticky tape to prevent this happening. They should be dark-coloured and preferably with rubber-covered fittings. Ideally they should be of a size that can be readily slipped into a pocket when not required and when slung round the neck require lens covers which are readily removed but not lost, i.e. connected to the glasses themselves. If they are worn round the neck it is advisable to be able to tuck them inside the jacket, shirt, or sweater, so that they do not get in the way when crawling. A useful tip is to fit an elastic-backed band to them in addition to the neck strap. If this is slipped round the chest it allows freedom to use them, but holds them neatly in position. They will come in for rough wear and usage in any event and, if expensive, are worth insuring against damage and loss. It is worth trying out as many as you can find and buying the best you can afford. Do not on any account, whatever you do, buy heavy great things which will impede your movements, however powerful they may be. Binoculars suitable for race-courses are anything but suitable for stalking.

The telescope

On the hill, or where long-distance viewing is possible, a telescope can undoubtedly prove its worth. It is by no means necessary to buy a new telescope since an old one which has been well looked after may often be obtained very cheaply and prove to be a considerable bargain. For scanning hillsides at long range and bringing deer at a distance into close focus they are undoubtedly hard to beat, even by the latest of binoculars, but they require considerable practice before they can be used effectively. They are also, like a telescopic sight and binoculars, not a great deal of use in the rain, although if they have a protective end sleeve that can be pulled out they are better than either of the others. Basically, however, in heavy rain, or mist, artificial aids to vision are useless.

The knife

It is up to everyone to make their own choice of knife when stalking, but a knife of sufficient size to gralloch a deer and, if necessary, give it its quietus is undoubtedly necessary. There are those who advocate carrying a large sheath knife strapped to the belt, others recommend a folding knife. Basically it depends on which you prefer. If you use a hard steel blade it is essential to keep it well sharpened and in this respect soft steel blades have the advantage that they are easily sharpened if necessary on any stone. If you do decide on carrying a folding blade make sure at least that it has a locking blade, or otherwise you may find yourself receiving a nasty cut. Whatever type of knife you do decide on using it is always advisable to have a lanyard connecting it to your belt, or wrist, when using it. Otherwise it is surprising how many times the knife will be left behind at the scene of the gralloch. I hate to admit how many times I have laid the knife aside after the gralloch and had to return for it at a later date. This can be a particularly annoying waste of time, so avoid it by attaching a lanyard to your knife.

Clothing

In any form of stalking the clothing should at the least match the background. Deer may be colour-blind, but even so it is undesirable to wear colours that clash violently with the background. Since it is easy today to buy government surplus camouflage smocks and trousers there is no need to look further for ideal camouflage clothing. New Zealand green wool smocks are also an ideal stalking top and Austrian loden cloth stalking capes are equally good. Both are designed for the job and for hard wear. The latter has the advantage that it is possible to carry a rifle and telescopic sight beneath it and keep them completely dry until the time comes for their use. On the other hand they are not ideal for crossing barbed-wire fences and in heavy rain eventually they do become waterlogged. On the other hand, it is highly undesirable to wear waxed waterproof cloth, however waterproof it may be, for it makes a continuous noise when brushing against twigs or branches, particularly when stalking in woodland, although really no better on the hill. Especially bad are the rustling nylon garments which make a swishing noise whenever one moves. They should be avoided like the plague.

Footwear

The question of what to wear on the feet must always depend to a large extent on the terrain. One thing that must always be anathema is wellington boots, which makes an appalling noise in woodland and are hopeless on the hill. On the hill, much again must depend on the type of ground. Studded boots, or commando-type rubber-soled boots, are both likely to be good in some places. I have known a pair of studded boots to lose all but two studs by the end of a day on rough going and a pair of commando boots to have lost more than a quarter of an inch (1.2 cm) of their half inch (2.5 cm) tread in similar conditions. Neither would have been desirable in woodland, where very often a pair of light dark-coloured gym shoes or jogging boots with light treads are best. An old kinsman of mine used to stalk barefoot, but his feet were calloused hard and this is not something to recommend unless your feet are in a similar condition. Undoubtedly, however, light shoes which will not squelch in wet conditions are best suited for woodland stalking. Heavy boots cracking branches underfoot, or wellingtons, are entirely wrong in such circumstances. Whatever you wear should be comfortable and well-worn and you should have at least one spare pair available while the others are drying.

Headgear and gloves

It is desirable to wear some form of hat to conceal the shape of the head on the hill and in forest stalking. A fore and after, or twa snouter, which can be tied down under the chin to keep rain off the back of the neck, as well as keeping the ears warm, has a lot to be said for it in cold conditions on the hill. Gloves, or mittens, which conceal the whiteness of the hands are also desirable in forest stalking. There are those who advocate face masks in woodland stalking, although as with any other form of stalking I have always felt that a handful of mud, or earth, smeared on the face will provide all the cover required. A face mask can become extremely warm and does nothing to keep away midges, whereas a handful of mud combines both to keep off midges and conceal the whiteness of the face. It is easily enough washed off at the end of the day.

Miscellaneous equipment

Compass and whistle
These are only really required on the hill, where it can happen that the mist comes down abruptly and even on familiar territory your sense of direction and whereabouts are easily lost. On those rare occasions the compass may make all the difference and should you be separated from your companion, or be completely lost and in need of help, the whistle can be at times a genuine lifesaver.

Knapsack and rope
An easily folded nylon knapsack can be carried in woodland stalking into which a roe may be placed, thus saving yourself from getting your clothes bloody. Whatever deer you may be stalking, a length of nylon rope some ten feet or so at least in length is another piece of equipment which should always be carried. Using this it is usually possible to haul any beast over the necessary distance between where it has been shot and where it can be lifted by a pony or vehicle.

Stick
There are two views on sticks. On the one hand there are those who consider they are essential, either on the hill or when woodland stalking. They can certainly be a help on the hill both in climbing and in steadying the telescope when spying the ground. They can also be used as a toggle to tow the beast during the haul. In either case they need to be strong and it is desirable they should not have a metal ferrule, which may clink against stones. In woodland stalking they can be used to support the rifle for a shot, either sitting, kneeling, or standing, but they require then to be about the same height as their owner, so that a standing shot can be taken comfortably. Again they can be used to act as a pole to carry a roebuck, or as a toggle when hauling a heavier beast to a track for the landrover to pick it up. This is another matter of individual preference.

Flask

Some whisky carried purely for medicinal purposes to restore the stalker's nerves when a deer has been shot is advisable on the hill. In woodland stalking it is only necessary to restore the circulation in conditions of extreme cold.

5

Stalking in Woodland and Open Hill

Part I

Woodland Stalking

Knowledge of the ground

The first essential in woodland stalking, as in any form of deer stalking, is to know the ground and the habits of the deer frequenting it. The initial requirement therefore on facing new ground is a large-scale map of the area. After studying it carefully and assessing the places in which deer will most likely be found, the next stage is examining the ground itself. It is probably advisable first to walk the boundaries and from there work into the centre, covering the ground carefully, with binoculars only, until you know it intimately. Each clearing in the woods, each well worn deer path through them, the views down the rides, the boggy patches, the new planting and the cleared ground, the areas of good natural feeding, the patches of thick cover, should all be investigated.

Signs of deer

While learning the ground in this way, naturally the stalker will be looking for any signs of deer. Any obvious deer runs should be investigated and any recent deer tracks seen on them should be carefully inspected. From the slots of the deer it is possible with experience to form a reasonably accurate idea not only of the species concerned but also of the age, sex, and numbers present. In the same way any droppings found should be examined and again a good idea of the species, age and size of the deer may be learned from them. Other signs such as anointing posts, fraying stocks, or scrapes, may indicate the size and age of the buck, or stag, making them. The height of the browse line in trees and bushes should be noted and again quite a lot can be learned from it regarding the species, size and numbers of deer present. Any special feeding places should be noted and any couches that are discovered where deer have been in the habit of lying up overnight, or during the day. All these signs should help to build up a picture of the deer on the ground, quite apart from any seen during these preliminary investigations.

Tracks
A brief description has already been given of what the slots and droppings of the various species of deer may look like. At first it is very easy to confuse them with the tracks of cloven-footed domestic animals, such as sheep and goats, or even cattle and pigs. It is probably advisable for a start to check the tracks and droppings of any such domestic cloven-footed animals in the area, particularly sheep, until you can identify these at a glance and eliminate them. Although only practice in tracking in the field will provide experience enough to tell the difference at once, the tracks of all species of deer are very different from those of domestic animals in several obvious ways;

1. They follow more or less in one central line. A doe, or hind, particularly will leave tracks which are almost exactly in one line. A buck, or stag, will also be closely aligned, but it is usually possible with an older beast at least to note that they are slightly more widely spaced. The tracks of domestic animals, with the exception of goats, tend to be much more widely spaced.

2. All deer tend to have the cleaves pointing in at the toes and the cleaves are only separated when moving fast, or on soft ground. All domestic cloven-footed animals tend to have the cleaves slightly separated, even at a walk.

3. In the case of deer the cleaves are pointed at the toe and rounded at the heel. Those of domestic animals tend to be more rounded and generally thicker, though again the goat is slightly exceptional but, even if thinner, it too is rounded at toe and heel.

In general, the differences are clear enough when comparisons are made on the ground, but only experience in tracking can train anyone to tell the differences more or less at a glance, even on strange ground.

Tracking
Just as the best way to learn the tracks of domestic animals is to follow them as they move around a field, or muddy area, so it is with deer. The best time for tracking them is after watching deer

retreating to cover soon after dawn. At almost any period of year tracks tend to show up then better than at any other time of the day. In snow, or hoar frost, of course, they are generally very clear, but tracks also show up very plainly in dew in early morning conditions, and they are especially easy to see in the light of a low rising sun. The tracks remain very clear for some time where the grass has been trodden and are easy to follow. As with freshly cut strips on a mown lawn, the tracks will appear light if followed, but dark if they are going in the opposite direction. They should be followed to the edge of the cover, where any creeps, or entries, should be checked. By following the cover round, if this is possible, and checking all likely places for any exit tracks, it may be feasible to learn where the deer are couched and to have a shrewd idea of their sex and numbers. With practice in checking all tracks seen in passes over streams and similar revealing muddy places, or in well worn deer paths in cover, as well as checking any droppings found, it is possible to build up a picture of the deer movements in the area. It is advisable, if possible, however, to find an experienced tutor in the early stages. This is not something that can readily be learned from the pages of any book and only constant practice and attention to detail will train anyone to track efficiently.

Vantage points
While walking round initially, the stalker should be mentally noting all suitable vantage points covering clearings or rides, from where it is likely a shot might be taken. It is especially important when examining the ground in this way to check and remember where all the nearest human habitations, or any public roads, or paths, are in relation to the ground. It is also always important at all times to note where any stock are grazing. It is no excuse after a shot has been taken and a prize Guernsey cow, or worse still its owner, has been shot, to say that you were not aware they were there. It is essential to know in advance where you are placing your bullets and where they might go should you miss. Safety First is the prime essential in all forms of shooting.

Safety margins
It is always important, if possible, to choose vantage points for shooting which are somewhat raised above the neighbouring ground so that you know that you have a safety margin, since you are firing downwards and can be sure your bullet, should you miss, will lodge harmlessly in the ground. In the same way rising ground

in the background, as long as it is free of stock, may also be served as a safe background, ensuring that a miss will not travel any distance, to the possible danger of some innocent person. Safety margins are one of the more important factors to bear in mind when prospecting any ground, especially if there are any roads or buildings in the neighbourhood. It always has to be remembered that a rifle bullet may travel over a mile and still be lethal. For this reason shots should never be taken at deer silhouetted against the skyline, however tempting they may appear. There may be stock, or people, unseen in the background where a miss might finally lodge. The chances of this happening may well be remote, but chances are not something that should be taken with a lethal weapon such as a rifle.

Neighbouring ground
It is as well to remember that deer can and often do cover considerable distances. It is important to consult the map and work out which of the neighbouring ground is likely to be attractive to them. Knowledge of your own ground will include knowledge of which neighbouring ground they are likely to find attractive and where they may from time to time withdraw. There are bound to be areas where beasts may wander sometimes considerable distances either side of the territorial boundaries. It is always as well to establish friendly relations and have a mutually agreed code of rules with your neighbours, regarding such matters as following a wounded beast over the boundary, or shooting close to the boundary. It may even be that it is desirable to come to a mutual agreement on the number of beasts culled over the combined areas for the benefit of both. In general, most people are agreeable to a fair arrangement in such matters so long as there is no danger of undue advantage being taken by either side.

Checking the deer
Once the ground has been thoroughly investigated and some idea formed of the number of deer present, it is then desirable to start stalking, but at first the object should not be to shoot deer, merely to learn more fully their numbers, territories and habits, so that selective shooting may follow. Simply to start shooting without any real knowledge of the deer on the ground is on a par with driving deer to groups of unskilled guns. It is true that an experienced person may be able to tell at a glance whether a beast is young, old, a buck in velvet, or a doe with fawn at foot, or similar quick assess-

Red hind

Roe doe

Sika hind

Fallow doe

Muntjac doe

ments, but unless the deer on the ground are known by previous observation it is still not possible to decide for certain whether the deer presenting themselves should be shot or not. To be sure whether an individual deer should be shot requires considerable time spent in merely observing them throughout the year. This is the essence of woodland stalking, but is also applicable to stalking in general.

The methods of stalking

Woodland stalking is very different from stalking on the open hill in that there is seldom any opportunity to see the quarry at a distance and make a prepared stalk over the intervening ground with an eye to shooting a particular beast. Selective shooting of individual beasts in woodland stalking, as indicated, requires considerable knowledge of the ground and also of the habits of the deer on it. Only by experience on the ground is it possible to ensure that you are culling those beasts which you wish to remove for the improvement of the stock and in the best interests of the forestry, or neighbouring farmland. Unfortunately these factors do not always coincide, although possibly more often than is sometimes realised.

The still-hunt
There are several methods of woodland deer stalking. The first of these is commonly termed the still-hunt, so-termed because the stalker remains in one place, generally concealed in a hide on the ground, or against a tree, or similar place of concealment, facing a clearing, or some such area with a good field of fire where he expects deer to be feeding. In the summer the hunter is liable to be eaten alive by flies and midges, when anti-midge spray is essential. In winter he is liable to be frozen solid in a short while, when a hand warmer is equally essential if a shot is to be taken effectively.

A common variant of the still-hunt is when the stalker is up the tree, sitting, or standing, in a suitable comfortable viewing position, either in a fork of the tree, or in a specially constructed high seat, termed in Germany a hoch-sitz, or hoch-platz, or, in big-game hunting, a machan.

The high seat, or deer platform
Like platforms for pigeon shooting, for which they may well be used on occasions if suitably placed, these may range from the lunatic to the palatial. They may be only a matter of twelve feet (3.5 m)

off the ground, or as much as thirty feet (9.2 m), or more, up in the tree-tops. There are many variations including readily portable versions, which have the advantage that they can be set up very readily and are easily moved if, for one reason or another, the first position is found to be unsuitable. A portable platform may consist of a ladder of light tubular steel with a small seat at the top, on the same principle as a child's high chair, which is readily roped, or strapped, to a suitable tree. A wooden construction on the same lines may also be made, or bought comparatively cheaply.

Alternatively a solid platform may be constructed in the top of a tree with a good field of view, or a more solid tower constructed, either of tubular steel scaffolding, or from wood. Such towers, however, usually require wire guy ropes to steady them, since otherwise in any sort of wind there is liable to be considerable sway, which makes them unsuitable for rifle shooting. The same is often true of those constructed in the treetops themselves. They may be perfectly all right for shooting pigeons in such circumstances, but for accurate rifle shooting they are hopeless, unless there is little or no wind. Whichever type of high seat is preferred it should be placed in position at least six months before it is intended to be used in order to accustom the deer to its presence. Apart from being considerably cheaper, the advantage of readily movable, as opposed to semi-permanent, structures is that in course of time trees and cover are likely to grow up and obscure the view. It is always important to keep the field of fire clear and wherever possible to remove any branches, or small trees, which may tend to obscure or constrict it, but when the growth has become too great the temporary high seats can easily be moved.

Siting
The siting of such hides, whether on the ground, or elevated, is all-important. They are frequently placed covering the intersections of rides in forestry, thus giving alternative fields of fire. They may also be on the edge of forestry covering likely feeding grounds, or clearings where deer are known to gather. They are generally placed so that they cover deer paths entering a favourite feeding place, or crossing point. They should not, however, be placed too close to such paths, for to have deer actually moving underneath, or too close at hand, makes for difficult shooting. It is far better to have them some thirty yards or so away, so that a broadside-on shot is likely to be presented. If they are too close to the deer path there is also the likelihood that the approaching deer will scent the trail the

stalker has left as he neared the hide. In every way therefore it is desirable to place these hides, whether on the ground or above it, some distance either side of any such recognised routes. If taking up a position on the ground near to any such deer path it is of course essential to be down-wind.

Still-hunting

Somewhat confusingly, still-hunting is also a term often used to describe very slow stalking on foot in woodland. In that a mile an hour is quite possibly too fast a rate of progression, it can be seen that the term is not entirely inapplicable. The all-important feature of still-hunting in woodlands is to avoid noise, or fast movement. Every piece of ground within view should be carefully checked with binoculars before moving another step. Each fresh piece of ground thus brought into view should again be checked. Progress may at first appear painfully slow, but as the stalker comes to recognise where to look and what to look for, he may find progress no faster, but the results more satisfactory.

Only experience can teach an individual an eye for deer. Distinguishing instantly the red body colouring showing through a paler patch of bracken, the white patch of the target moving, the tell-tale movement of an antler over a bush, or the twitch of an ear at an irksome fly, is all part of the stalker's craft which only comes with practice. Such give-away signs as these are only immediately recognised after many months of observation. Even then, only too often, the first thing seen is the familiar shape of the head of a doe, or hind, gazing suspiciously towards you with ears cocked. The only thing to do then is freeze instantly and hope the beast will start grazing again, having only just caught sight of you at the same moment you caught sight of it. In practice it is surprising how often this must happen. One is conscious of being watched while slowly scanning the surroundings and there suddenly is a deer looking enquiringly at you where there was nothing visible a moment earlier. That is the moment to freeze solid, for the chances are that as you have just discovered it, so it has just observed something suspicious and may still not be certain what you are. It is surprising how often in such circumstances deer will continue feeding after a few minutes. If they remain suspicious they may attempt the trick common to most deer when uncertain of something suspicious of appearing to continue feeding casually while moving round to catch the wind. Once they have the scent, of course, they are gone.

The only way in which deer can be seen and recognised in time, before they have detected the presence of the stalker and departed, is by carefully and thoroughly searching the ground with the binoculars. It is thus easy to appreciate that the pace of still-hunting is extremely slow and the more experienced the still-hunter the slower he is likely to move. A good comparison might be made with the fisherman who casts over the river in front of him methodically, with increasingly lengthy casts, until he has covered all the water, sometimes covering a likely area more than once, and only then takes a step forward to repeat the process again. By the nature of things, since deer are generally already out feeding before dawn, to go to the high seat then would merely mean disturbing them to no purpose. Thus, the still-hunt is more likely to take place in the evening, whereas still-hunting is more generally practiced at dawn.

Identification

Once the deer has been seen, the next and most important stage of the still-hunt, or of still-hunting, is to identify it clearly. There have been cases of stalkers who have seen a patch of red and lined up their sights only to discover at the last moment that they were about to shoot a Hereford bull. Make sure at the very least therefore that you can see the deer clearly and preferably so that you can identify it as one you wish to cull. Only after clear identification should you consider raising the rifle and then it is equally essential that you do not shoot unless you have a clear view for a killing shot. This again may involve a considerable wait, but that is part of the scheme of things in still-hunting. As with the static still-hunt, it is very often a case of patiently letting the deer do the work and come to you, rather than trying to approach them more closely.

Although in the normal course of events only one person is likely to be present in a still-hunt, or when still-hunting, it is sometimes necessary where a 'rifle' does not know the ground for a stalker to go with him as a guide. The stalker will naturally take the lead and indicate where and when to expect a deer, also which are the beasts to be shot and which to be left. If the 'rifle' is sufficiently experienced, he may be allowed to take the lead when still-hunting, but by the nature of things the man who knows the ground always has the advantage in finding deer first, since he knows from experience where to look and the most likely places to find them. It is, of course, possible to enjoy either form of the still-hunt with a well-tried partner, taking it in turns to be stalker and 'rifle'. A spirit of healthy competition in such circumstances can help to sharpen the senses and it is always helpful to have two to carry the deer, once shot. These are, however, not the only methods of woodland stalking, for the drive can also be very effective at times. (See p. 102).

The Seasons

The different seasons have an immense effect on woodland stalking. Far greater in many ways than on the hill.

Winter
In the winter when the trees are bare of leaf and the undergrowth is sparse, woodland stalking may provide much longer-range shots. It is possible then to see the deer at much greater distances and, of course, conversely, they can see the stalker. Winter stillness also makes for much more noise, as sound travels clearly in cold still air. The crunching of feet on snow, or frosty ground, carries a long way. Then too, it is desirable to be well clad against the chill resulting from standing still for long periods in freezing temperatures. On the other hand, windy conditions are also common enough in the winter months and full advantage may be taken of them, since the deer are at a disadvantage in that their hearing is considerably handicapped and the careful stalker can often get very close in such conditions.

Spring
As the growth begins and dawn starts ever earlier the stalker can take full advantage of the longer hours available. The roebucks in velvet may be watched with interest as they start to rub it off and reveal their new antlers and try them out on saplings. Shooting at this time should generally be restricted to culling any poor specimens it is desired to get out of the way.

Summer
With the foliage on the trees and the undergrowth fully grown, stalking is difficult in woodland, although at various levels it may be effective. From above in a high seat, or peering below the undergrowth at the level of a deer's head when grazing, it is often possible to see beasts in cover. On the whole, however, the main shots are likely to be taken in the open when deer are feeding at dawn and dusk. Midges and flies may well be an occupational hazard and shirt sleeves worn long are desirable.

Autumn
With the undergrowth dying down and the leaves beginning to
vanish the 'Fall' is the finest time in many ways for stalking. The
season spent watching the deer develop, at play and rutting, can

now be used to cull those beasts it is felt should go for the benefit of the stock on the ground. With the antlers free of velvet it is possible to assess the heads and identify with reasonable certainty the various beasts which should be culled.

Fallow deer on the edge of a wood

The weather

The effects of certain weather conditions on woodland stalking are fairly predictable. Thus a full moon and cloudless sky overnight will mean that the deer have been feeding freely throughout the hours of semi-darkness and will retire to lie up very soon after dawn. The stalker who wishes to stalk after such a night may well find that many of the beasts he would expect to find have already departed.

On the other hand, a cloudy overcast night when the moon is not to be seen will probably mean that at dawn the deer are trying to make up for the lack of feeding opportunities overnight. During moonless periods it is less important what type of weather it has been, for again the deer will be forced to feed from first light until they have had sufficient feeding to retire. Thus the stalker may expect a reasonably long period when deer may be seen at dawn and may expect them to come out early at dusk. The ideal conditions for the woodland stalker are thus when the night has been overcast, or moonless, with a fresh breeze blowing in the morning. Then the deer are eager to feed and their hearing is handicapped, so that the stalker may well approach much closer than normal without being detected.

Part II

Factors Common to Woodland and Open Ground Stalking

Deer driving from woodland into open ground

Unlike the method of deer driving whereby an area of wood is surrounded by inexperienced shooters armed with shot guns, deer driving to a waiting rifle can often be very effective, as well as selective. Like most forms of stalking, however, it is something of a lottery in that deer seldom do what is expected of them and in this lies half the attraction of deer stalking in any form. In this case the principle is simple enough. A deer, or group of deer, are known to be found usually in a certain area at a certain time. It may be advisable to check by tracking that they are in the expected place, but where knowledge of the ground and the habits of the deer are sufficiently well known this may not be necessary. A rifle is posted in a suitably commanding position down wind, covering the exits the deer are most likely to take. The driver then enters the wood at the opposite side and, without haste, gradually drives the wood to the waiting rifle. If he zig-zags gently and unhurriedly through the ground and knows the pattern of movement of the deer the likelihood is that the deer will immediately catch his wind and move ahead of him out of the wood, taking, if all goes well, the path that was intended. The deer should then emerge quietly in full view of the waiting rifle, providing him with ample opportunity to select the deer desired from any small family group.

This form of driving can be eminently satisfactory, although, naturally enough, it cannot always be guaranteed to work, but with a thorough knowledge of the deer movements in the area it should normally be effective enough. It is always pleasing for a stalker who knows the ground really well to be able to put a rifle in position and indicate exactly where a certain deer is likely to appear and even to forecast where it is likely to halt and where to shoot it. The sound of the shot is then usually a source of considerable inward satisfaction.

Two-way driving
A similar method may also be used with two rifles working in conjunction with each other. It is essential here that each knows exactly where the other will be moving so that there is no possible danger of either of them firing a shot which might conceivably be in the direction of the other. The principle in effect is that each is still-hunting in his ground, with the intention that any deer startled by the one will move into the other's territory. Should any deer be moved by this method it is sometimes useful to be able to signal to each other, if conditions allow for it. This may be either by a loud whistle, a horn, or by a walkie-talkie. Short wave radio can be very useful sometimes, but if there is any danger of alerting deer it is better by far to stick to a code of whistles, keeping them to an absolute minimum. In all forms of stalking the less noise made the better. The sound of a shot is usually signal enough in itself and on hearing one fired the other stalker should immediately prepare himself for the possible approach of deer in his direction.

Attracting deer

In any form of stalking there are occasions when the deer's attention can be usefully attracted. At the lowest level it is often worth giving a sharp whistle, or a loud imitation bark, when a deer has seen you and is about to take flight, or even when it is bounding away. This may often have the effect of arousing its curiosity to the point where it stops and presents an opportunity for a shot. When the stalker's presence is suspected and the deer is uneasy, but still uncertain, a bark, or a bleat as of a fawn or calf, or an in-season doe or hind, may well have the effect of attracting the beast's attention and causing it to stand still in a suitable position for a shot. Where a deer can be heard in thick undergrowth, but cannot be seen, these tactics may sometimes have the effect of bringing it into the open.

The use of a call, such as can be bought in most gunsmiths', is quite helpful on such occasions. Indeed, many people who have tried calling roebucks in the rut by using such a call may well agree it is sometimes even more effective in such circumstances. To judge by my own experience, to call a buck during the rut is largely a matter of luck. I have been instructed by an expert Austrian caller, whose advice was that one should blow three or four quick calls at about three- or four-second intervals, each towards a different point of the compass, thus imitating the doe circling round in the way they do. He maintained that the buck could hear this and home in on it unerringly. Unfortunately the results, when I have tried it, have not justified his faith in the method.

There are those who advocate calling by using a leaf, or a piece of grass, between the hands, or else simply sucking the back of the hand. I have called stoats and foxes by this method, which closely resembles the scream of a terrified rabbit, but to me at least the sound does not resemble a roe doe calling enticingly. In any event everyone appears agreed on one thing and that is that, whatever method of calling is used, it is inadvisable to repeat it too often or roe may be driven off the ground. Unless conditions are very suitable it is obvious that a lot of luck must be involved in calling the required buck to the required spot at the required time. There are simply too many outside factors involved, but then, of course, there is no certainty in any form of stalking, which is half the attraction of the sport.

Since this form of calling is limited to about six weeks or so in each year, somewhat naturally very few people have any great experience of success with it. In spite, or perhaps because, of this, most people are prepared to persevere even without any great expectation of success. In my own experience, such a call used at any time of the year can have the effect of checking the roe of either sex, much as a well-imitated bark may also do. When poised on the brink of flight any unexpected noise, including, as indicated, a sharp whistle, may also have the effect of causing the deer to hold still for a vital moment or two to allow sufficient time for a shot to be taken.

Calling a stag during the rut in woodland can also be effective. By imitating the 'roar' the stag may well be induced to come towards the sound. Hindered by the necessity to keep his hinds suitably herded, the process may be a lengthy one, but none the less both satisfying and exciting. Sika, too, may be attracted in a similar way, but fallow bucks will not pay any attention to such attempts to lure them.

The American method of rattling bones to imitate bucks fighting at the height of the rut could well be effective in this country too, although I have never heard of it being used. In general, the curiosity of deer is something that can often be used to attract them. Any strange noise at the right moment can cause them to pause for long enough to allow a shot.

When a deer is lying down, either in cover or in the open, there is often the problem of waiting for it to rise. It may be that only the antlers can be seen, while the rest of the deer is concealed, or it may be that only a portion of the deer is visible and a certain shot cannot be taken. Waiting then can often be a lengthy business and should the wind alter, or another deer approach, the stalker may be discovered and the wait wasted as the deer leaps to its feet and departs at a gallop. In such circumstances some people advocate whistling to attract the deer's attention and this can often be effective, but it can also alarm the deer and cause it to take off at speed. A better method, to my mind, is to try to imitate some natural sound which arouses its curiosity. Thus an imitation of the bleat of a fawn or calf, the sound of the mating call, or even a bark may be effective. Like so much in deer stalking, what may work perfectly with one deer on one occasion may prove worse than useless on another occasion with a different animal, even in what may seem exactly similar circumstances. That, of course, is one of the fascinations of stalking.

Estimating range

The shot when stalking in woodland may vary from as little as 10 yards (9.2 m) to around an average of 70 yards (64.7 m). Shots of much over that range are unusual, but when shooting at deer feeding on the edge of woodland it may sometimes be necessary to take a shot at around 100–150 yards (92–138 m). Even in open ground, shots over 150–200 yards (138–184 m) should be left, unless the beast has been wounded and it is essential that it is shot.

A good way to estimate range is, as indicated earlier, by using the graticules in a fixed telescopic sight, if you have one fitted with them. Even so it is always desirable to be used to estimating range without aids of this kind. One method is to accustom yourself to some definite length, such as a cricket pitch, which is 22 yards (20 m). Any object 'two cricket pitches' away is about 45–50 yards (41–45.5 m); doubled, the distance is around 90–100 yards (82–93 m). Another method is to pace out 50 yards (45.5 m) and memorise that distance. Then try to estimate it again and pace it out once more. By frequently estimating a range when out walking and checking it by pacing the distance out, it becomes second nature to estimate ranges reasonably accurately. If, whenever a deer is shot, an estimate is\made of the range and the distance is then paced, this again will make for accuracy in estimating range. It should be remembered, however, that when shooting across a valley it is easy to underestimate range.

The field of fire

One of the most important aspects of woodland stalking is ensuring that any shot taken is clear of any intervening branches or twigs, which may deflect the bullet. When stalking in woodland there are more cases of apparent misses or, worse still, wounded beasts, because of this than any other reason. Unless you have an absolutely clear view it is preferable not to shoot at all. It may often be tempting to shoot when you appear to have a clear view of various portions of the body, although not the whole beast, but it is preferable whenever possible to wait for a clear view and a certain killing shot.

Even when shooting in the open it is important to ensure that any shot taken is not likely to be deflected. Especially when shooting from a prone position it is quite easy to fail to realise that a small mound near the rifle barrel, or a clump of heather or just tall grass, is going to be in the way of the bullet, even though the telescopic sights give a clear field of fire. On one occasion, firing at a young buck in Dorset downland on the edge of Hampshire, I fired downhill and was chagrined to see the buck lurch forwards but fail to fall. Fortunately, confused by the echo from behind it, the beast limped up the hill towards me. A second shot appeared to have no visible effect, but then I realised that the waving grass in front of the barrel, though not visible through the telescopic sight, was deflecting the bullet. I rose at once and fired a hurried kneeling shot, which missed. Fortunately I was able to run downhill and come out below the buck which was standing broadside on further up the hill. A final standing shot put a quick and painless end to it, but not without the farmer making some caustic comments on the 'battue'.

Ensuring a clear shot
It is always important when aiming at a deer to ensure that no other beast is standing on the far side of it, for it can very easily happen that the shot kills the chosen deer, but goes on through it and wounds the deer behind it. This is especially the case in woodland stalking, when a doe may have a youngster almost hidden from view on the side away from the stalker. The same point holds good on the hill in the open when several deer are grouped together. It is essential then to wait until the chosen beast is completely clear of the others and there is no danger of the bullet going on to wound a second deer unintentionally. The same point, of course, applies when a deer is seen feeding amongst cattle or sheep. Whenever using a rifle it is imperative to bear in mind where the bullet may end up in such circumstances, whether the target is hit or missed.

Use of echoes
It is always worth noting whenever ground is likely to produce an echo. As in the instance noted above, any animals, including deer, can be very easily confused by an echo. It is sometimes possible to turn deer that have been on the point of running away by using an echo in this way. On other occasions a deer may turn when a companion is shot and run towards the rifle instead of away. By deliberately using an echo it is sometimes possible to persuade deer to move past a waiting rifle.

Using telescope, binoculars and telescopic sight correctly
The telescope, if used, is required for long range on the hill or open ground and can bring distant deer within focus so that shootable beasts may be picked out. The binoculars, if fitted with a zoom lens, may be almost capable of the same job, but basically they should be used for checking the ground immediately ahead, chiefly in woodland stalking, but also on the hill, although in poor light at dawn, or dusk, they are generally more effective.

The telescopic sight should only be used when the stalk is virtually completed and the shot is about to be taken. When woodland stalking it is undesirable to see a stalker constantly raising the rifle to look down the telescopic sight in order to glass the ground ahead. Unnecessary movement in this way can easily alert deer. Apart from that there is usually a loaded rifle involved and it can be downright dangerous. If that shadow ahead should be a man under a tree it is perfectly acceptable to look at him through binoculars, but quite another matter to point a loaded rifle at him. This is a sloppy and dangerous habit. Avoid it.

Part III

Stalking on Mainly Open Upland Ground

General principles

There is not really a great deal of difference between open ground stalking in, for instance, the Scottish Uplands in Dumfriesshire and Galloway, the Lake District, or the Hampshire and Dorset down-lands, or for that matter the Devon hills and moorland. The same general principles apply also in stalking in the highlands of Scotland on a deer forest which may appear at first sight to be little more than a barren boulder-strewn mountainside rising to over 3,000 feet (914 m). In each case the principle is to glass the ground ahead and to climb to a suitable vantage point on the high ground and spy out the land from there. In each case there are liable to be large amounts of dead ground caused by valleys, or false crests, where deer may be concealed from view, either from below or from above. As in every form of stalking, a sound knowledge of the ground is a first essential and, as with woodland stalking, the man who knows his ground well also knows where the deer are likely to be at any given season of the year and whatever the weather conditions.

Where the stalking area is not mountainous highland deer forest, but is mainly hilly ground, with many corresponding valleys, including a few copses, or wooded glens, it is ideal for all species of deer and may combine woodland stalking with open ground stalking. The difficult feature of such ground can be to know what deer are on it. This can only be achieved by careful reconnaissance. Stalking the ground with binoculars and/or telescope both outside the woodland and in it will be the only way to be sure of the deer population. An estimate may also be made by assessing the slots in muddy river crossings and similar places. Such traces may be the only indications to be found of some cunning old beasts. Some deer, especially old bucks or stags, may seldom stir out of the woodland.

Since very often an area in the centre of the ground is deliberately retained as a sanctuary, this can complicate matters. Much open ground stalking in such areas may at times take place in conjunction with woodland stalking. Indeed, in many parts of the country the two are closely connected, for it is common enough to find rolling, hilly ground planted with woodland to a considerable height. In such countryside the evening and dawn stalks may start from points of vantage where a good view of any deer feeding in the open can be obtained and from which a stalk can be quickly planned and executed. Unlike stalking in wide open hill ground or in a deer forest in the highlands there will only be a very limited time available for such stalks. On the other hand, it is often possible to make a comparatively quick and easy advance under cover of adjoining woodland to a suitable point for a shot. Once again knowledge of the ground is all-important.

Knowledge of the ground

As with woodland stalking, open upland stalking requires initially a sound knowledge of the ground, which with a large area often cannot be gained inside a year or even two and may require several seasons. In the case of some highland deer forests it is often inherited knowledge, in that the chief stalker has spent years on the ground as man and boy, following in his father's footsteps. It is simply impossible in the space of one or two seasons to gain the sort of intimate knowledge such a man often has of an area which may possibly extend to something like five or more square miles (8 km^2) of rocky mountainside, getting to know the formation of the ground and every wind eddy, as well as the deer population living on it or liable to pass over it.

In the case of the larger highland estates, the seasonal visiting stalker/rifle who visits such ground merely on an annual basis, as many landowners are forced to do by circumstance, cannot hope to learn sufficient to conduct a stalk over it effectively until he has had at least a couple of season's experience on the ground. On the other hand, it may be reasonable enough on such ground to pick a deer from a herd as one which should be shot, while on a woodland stalk picking a deer which should be shot might require a year at least of preparation. This is one of the big differences between open ground stalking and woodland stalking.

In both cases it is essential to know the ground thoroughly, but on open hill ground, especially in the Scottish highlands, even when accustomed to the terrain it is very easy to get lost in a sudden mist in the hills. Hazards of this nature are virtually unknown in woodland stalking, where one man by himself is more common than two together. On the hill two is not only more common, but infinitely more desirable. Whenever venturing on the hill, for climbing, walking, or deer stalking, it is always sensible, as a matter of common sense and safety first, to have a companion. To get lost on the hill when a mist comes down, or in an unexpected blizzard, is only too easy, even when you think you know the ground well. To be alone in such circumstances is not only highly undesirable, but downright foolish. If an ankle is twisted, or a limb broken, as can only too easily happen, the companion can go for help and assistance may readily be obtained. Without a companion, at best it might be necessary to pass an uncomfortable night and it has been known only too often for a death to result from loss of blood or exposure. The mountains of Scotland should never be underestimated and it is foolish to treat them lightly, for they are capable of sudden changes of weather from deceptive warmth to sub-arctic blizzard conditions which can catch even the experienced by surprise.

The deer on the ground
With knowledge of the ground on upland stalking to some extent inevitably comes a knowledge of the deer also, since when covering the ground it is possible to view the deer from a considerable distance. Of course this implies the intention to look for deer. It would be possible to walk such ground, as with woodland, and imagine there were no deer present. Knowledge of deer, recognition of their slot marks, droppings, hairs in wallows, scrapes and anointing posts, are all signs of the presence of deer to the knowledgeable stalker on the hill as in woodland, although slot marks are less likely to show on stony hill ground. With the aid of a telescope, or binoculars, however, it is possible on the hill in upland stalking to keep an eye on the deer themselves for a large part of the year with a comparative ease which is quite at variance with conditions in woodland.

Vantage points
On every hill there are certain places where the stalker knows in advance that a good view of the surrounding countryside can be

obtained. In all upland stalking the rule is to glass the hill at the start and then to head for the high ground. From above it is possible to look down on deer feeding in the lower ground, but with false crests and dead ground there are often surprisingly few places where good long-range views may be had over clear ground. As with woodland stalking it requires experience to pick out the deer against their natural background even when they are lying in full view in the open.

Neighbouring ground

As with woodland stalking, it is important in upland stalking, or in a highland deer forest, to know the boundaries well and the attractions of the neighbouring ground. Should you be unfortunate enough to wound a beast which takes refuge on neighbouring ground, the normal practice in the highlands is to let your neighbours know about it on your return to the lodge, so that they may look out for it. It is also usually customary, if a beast is close to the march, that a mutual arrangement known as 'stalker's law' operates, by which it is permissible to stalk as far as may be required to hide the stalker while crawling on hands and knees in order to take a shot, but too much advantage should never be taken of such agreements. Friendly relations with neighbours are always advisable.

Checking the deer population

This is generally a much simpler proposition than it is in thick woodland, although where there is any woodland involved – and plenty of hill ground has a fair amount – this may make matters more difficult than where the ground is entirely open. Another factor in open ground stalking is always the point that transient populations of deer may well complicate the issue. It is because of this that deer forests in the highlands are usually termed stag forests, or hind forests. If the bulk of the ground is that favoured by the hinds, then during the rut the stags will appear and the stalking will have all the added excitement involved at this period. In a stag forest, on the other hand, there are usually a large number of stags present with quite a few still in velvet early in the season and it is frequently very difficult to get near them. The stags will be on the high ground to avoid the midges and flies on the low ground, so it may well involve considerable walking to get near the beast of your choice and it is easy on a small forest to clear the ground unless you are very careful.

To a great extent the same factors control the movements of both fallow and sika. The roe on open ground may provide very interesting stalking indeed at a time when no other deer may be shot and have a knack of vanishing apparently into thin air, which on apparently open ground sometimes almost savours of witchcraft.

The methods of stalking

In almost any form of hill stalking over open ground it is important to present as small a target to the deer as possible. Therefore it is always advisable to advance in Indian file, rather than line abreast. It is, of course, important to remember that movement on the skyline is liable to attract the attention of deer below and alarm them. It is by no means always easy to say what is the skyline to deer on lower ground, since a false crest may well be the skyline to them. It is important therefore to keep glassing the ground in front to make sure there are no deer to whom you might be visible. If it is possible to approach from downwind, of course, it is always desirable to do so, but it may be necessary to approach at an angle to the wind. Whatever approach is made, it is always advisable to keep an eye on the ground ahead and note through the glass which way any grass or heather may be blowing with the wind. In the highland corries especially, the wind at one level may sometimes be blowing diametrically opposite to that at another.

If it is possible to advance out of the sun this will give the stalker a considerable advantage. When doing so, however, it is important to remember that a long shadow may be cast in front and the sight of it moving may alarm the deer, especially when cast across a glen onto the opposite hillside. If you should come unexpectedly on deer do not immediately drop flat, as sudden movement is more likely to attract their attention and alarm them. Freeze at first, then sink slowly to the ground and it is possible you may not alarm them. It is important never to make any hasty movements when close to deer and if the stalker in front freezes at the sight of deer raising their head then it is imperative to freeze also, even if in the middle of a stream.

When crawling, it is important not to have your buttocks high in the air, but to keep flat. Crawl flat on the ground with your head as the highest point. When going uphill crawl head first, but when going downhill crawl feet first. As with woodland stalking always make sure of the ground ahead of you as you advance. Deer are often lying in hollows where you did not expect them and once deer are on the move that is the stalk finished. One deer moving in alarm will take with it all the others on the hill, unlike woodland stalking where one deer moving may not necessarily disturb others.

Theoretically the higher you climb, the greater the area over which you may see deer, but, of course, this is not strictly true since false crests and dead ground may well leave a considerable number of deer unseen, however high you climb. Unless you are accustomed to the hill and very fit do not, however, try to keep up with your stalker, who, even if he is older than you, will be accustomed to the hill and to setting and keeping up a faster pace than you can hope to emulate. Take your time and do not hurry, for he will wait for you. Remember that when it comes to the stalk you may not only have to crawl long distances, you may also have to run at full speed over open ground or along a steep hillside. There is a long day to get through and there is no sense in being worn out before you are half way through it.

A normal stalk on the hill

Unlike the dawn or dusk routine of woodland stalking, the normal stalk in the Scottish highlands starts between 8.00 and 9.00 in the morning. The stalker and the 'rifle' then foregather and a practice shot or two may be taken at a target. This is not merely to test the accuracy of rifle and telescopic sight, but also to reassure both stalker and 'rifle'. After initially glassing the hill, the party then set off with the stalker leading, carrying the rifle, and the 'rifle' behind him.

The first stage may be spent in climbing upwards of 1,500 to 2,500 feet (461–769 m), to get well above the deer and in a position to spy the ground it is intended to stalk. Once a suitable herd of deer are sighted with a shootable beast amongst them the next stage is to gauge the wind and decide how to approach them. The stalker has to be in total command of the operation so far since the 'rifle' probably does not know the ground well enough, if at all, and has no real idea, even when the deer have been sighted, how the wind is likely to be blowing in the numerous valleys, or corries, of the mountainside beneath them. The stalker, on the other hand, from years of experience, should be able to assess the best line of approach and set about getting close to the deer at once by the best possible line. Once the stalker has worked out his chosen line of approach, mentally noting various boulders, patches of heather or similar landmarks on the way, he may, or may not, explain to the 'rifle' his reasoning and the route he is proposing to take, if he thinks he has time to do so before the beasts have moved. In any event he will then lead the way from the point where the deer were seen, by means of a concealed approach to a position downwind, where the stalk can begin.

Depending entirely on where the deer are placed, the final stalk may be easy or difficult, resulting in a wet crawl along the centre of a burn, or a simple approach to a boulder on the edge of a hill. The stalker, as explained, at his first viewing will have worked out the line of approach and decided on the best route and simplest stalk from downwind, but once this stage has been reached, there may be unforeseen factors, such as grazing sheep, or hinds, in the way. It is also easy to get disorientated and lose the landmarks noted from above so that the wrong line is taken. This should not happen with a stalker who knows his ground well, but it is not something that can be achieved without at least a year or more on the ground and an experienced eye for the hill ground.

Although a stalk such as the one described might be achieved by a reasonably experienced 'rifle' it is more likely that in attempting it all the deer would be driven over the march onto the neighbouring territory. Alternatively the stalk might be made and the deer would be found to have already long departed, having taken alarm on receiving the wind of the stalker at an early stage in the stalk, owing to his lack of knowledge of the wind currents in the area. Stalking on strange ground, especially in a deer forest in the highlands, is simply not something that can be left to a person who does not know the ground intimately, not least because of the unintentional damage he may cause in unwittingly scaring deer off the ground. After returning at the end of their first day as darkness is falling, with or without a stag, even the most obstinate and self-opinionated egotists will probably be prepared to agree that this is so. Notwithstanding this, it may be that after the initial stalk the stalker gains sufficient confidence in the ability of the 'rifle' to let him lead at some point in ensuing stalks and, naturally, this makes for greater interest for all concerned, even if a stag should be lost as a result.

The deer passes

Stalking deer in the Scottish highlands and in upland ground also involves shooting hinds during the winter months, which can be a very wearing experience. As indicated, the older hinds are very experienced in the ways of man and they can prove extremely alert and hard to stalk. One method of killing off these old hinds is by two or three stalkers working in concert. The old hinds will lead the way over the deer paths and over particular deer passes in the hills which have been used for centuries. A knowledge of these is essential to the highland stalker. If one or more rifles are placed in position covering these passes while another shows himself and gently drives the deer into position, then a number of old hinds may be killed with comparative ease. Knowing at what distance the sight of a human being will not alarm deer unduly, and where they are likely to move having regard to the ground and the wind, can only be learned by experience on the ground, as with driving in woodland stalking. There is still then the problem of hauling them off the hill, which may not always prove a simple task.

The seasons

In some ways the advantages of the seasons are reversed in open ground stalking, as opposed to woodland stalking.

Winter
When the cold winds of November start blowing over open ground the one advantage is that it may be possible to use them to stalk up unobserved on deer sheltering from them in the hollows. Freezing weather on the hill, especially when waiting for deer to move, somehow usually seems worse than in the comparative shelter of woodland. Snow and ice on the hill can also make for worse conditions for stalking than in woodland and are likely to bring the deer down to the lower ground.

Spring
With the longer dawns and later dusk, stalking in open ground can be very interesting, with or without a rifle. The arrival of the calves and fawns makes for interesting stalking and provides plenty of opportunity for the camera. Once the roebucks are clear of velvet from April onwards they too may provide good sport and as good stalking over open ground as any deer.

Summer
With the summer, when flies and midges make a repellent essential, stalking can be very interesting. With plenty of cover still avail-

able on the woodland edges and the deer just approaching the rut, this can be a good time for stalking. The roebucks can also provide excellent sport.

Autumn
Here again is the ideal time of the year for stalking most deer. With the confusion and excitement of the rut, deer stalking on the open hill has a dimension all its own.

The weather

There is little point in going out when the hills are shrouded in misty rain so that visibility is no more than a few feet. Equally it is desirable not to go out in seemingly fine weather and be suddenly caught in such conditions on the highest part of the deer forest. Returning unscathed in such conditions can sometimes be more a matter of luck than judgement. Heavy thunderstorms on the hill can also be quite frightening and when lightning is flickering about it is desirable to have the rifle encased in a sleeve. When high winds are blowing, the deer will be unpredictable and jumpy, and on the whole it is better to stay at home. The deer themselves are probably the best barometer available and if they are seen coming down to shelter a spell of bad weather is assured, whatever the weather forecasters may say.

6

The Shooting and The Shot

Using the Rifle

Because a person can fire at a target and hit the bull every time at various ranges it is easy to think that when faced with a large target such as a deer he could not possibly miss. The facts, unfortunately, are very different for he may well not even hit it, let alone kill it. The difference between lying comfortably at full length on a firing range with a target rifle and the often extremely uncomfortable positions one is forced to adopt when stalking can be very great indeed, quite aside from the undoubted psychological difference of aiming at a live target.

I have to admit that I am not a very good shot at target practice and I know several other people I would rely on to kill deer, who are no better. The fact is that there is an enormous difference between a large, possibly moving, live target in the wild and a small static one on the range. Admittedly, I do know some excellent rifle shots who are as good when stalking as they are on the range, but the two performances are by no means identical. They are indeed very different. In the same way as clay pigeon shooting differs from live pigeon shooting and the expert at one may not be good at the other, so it is with target shooting and shooting deer.

Sighting in the telescopic sight

Before shooting it is essential to ensure that the rifle and the telescopic sight are correctly sighted in. When it comes to zeroing the telescopic sight a sight aligner, as indicated, is a great saver of time and ammunition. If one is not available, a useful tip is to carve two notches in the top sides of a wooden box and set the rifle in them some twenty yards from a target set up against a suitable background, where bullets cannot ricochet, or cause damage. By removing the bolt the rifle can then be bore-sighted by peering down the barrel and aiming at the bull. The telescopic sight should then be aimed at the bull also. Then fire a bullet at the target and see where it hits. Make the necessary adjustments and you should then be about ready. Fire another shot, which should be on target. Then fire a group at twenty-five yards making any further adjustments necessary and finally another at a hundred. Both should be firmly on target, giving you at least a reasonable grouping. Thereafter you should have no need to worry about your rifle unless the telescopic sight receives a knock. If this happens, or you have an improbable miss, it is advisable to re-sight your rifle in case the sight has been knocked off its correct alignment or, worse still, has been damaged. If, for instance, the graticules have been loosened this may be quite difficult to check, as the groupings will be all over the place regardless of where you adjust the sight. A sight aligner saves a great deal of time and trouble, as well as ammunition.

Preparation and practice

Practice in field conditions is essential, however good with a rifle you may be on the range. To my mind, one of the best ways of training oneself to stalk and shoot deer is to stalk rabbits with a .22. The comparison may sound absurd, but the practice is almost identical, at least in the case of woodland shooting. If you have the opportunity to stalk rabbits at dawn or in the evening there are few better ways of training for stalking deer. If you can guarantee to stalk within a distance of 30 yards (28 m) or so of a feeding rabbit and shoot it with a .22, that is good training. If you can pull off a shot with a .22 at a moving rabbit at around the same distance you should be able to cope with any shot at deer that is likely to arise. The essence of stalking is to know where to put your bullet and to put it there or nearly there as often as possible. If the opportunity does not arise for a certain killing shot, then it is better to leave it for another day.

Carrying the rifle safely

As a matter of course the rifle should never be carried with a cartridge in the chamber unless you are about to start a stalk. It is never wise to rely on the safety catch.

By all means carry four cartridges in the magazine, but keeping the spring of the magazine under constant stress with a full charge of five cartridges is liable to cause faulty cartridge feeding after a while.

Never in any circumstances carry the rifle at the trail; the muzzle should always be pointing directly upwards or to the ground.

The best way to carry a rifle for any distance is slung over the back of the shoulder. When starting a woodland stalk however it will be found useful to reverse this and carry it slung over the left shoulder (if shooting from the right side) with the barrel inside. With practice it is then only the work of a second or two at most to slide the rifle forward so that the elbow supports the sling and the rifle is braced for a shot.

Another common method is to carry the rifle over the left shoulder with the muzzle pointing downwards and the butt uppermost, but with this method there is a danger of getting dirt in the muzzle should you trip.

When approaching the end of a stalk in woodland the high port, with the elbow through the sling, will have you at maximum readiness, but the shot itself should never be hurried. This merely gives you more time to prepare for it coolly and methodically. Any haste over the actual shot is to be avoided as only one step away from buck fever.

Buck fever

Buck fever, as it is so aptly termed, is one of the complications which can attack almost anyone at times when stalking. Even experienced shots can be affected. It is something that is only really overcome by an attitude of mind and by constant practice. Daily practice in front of a mirror, if nothing better is available, is thus always worth while. When it comes to shooting and stalking deer, if you are used to raising your rifle and sighting and taking a shot without conscious effort regardless of the circumstances, whether sitting, kneeling, lying or standing, you are immediately better placed than the person who is only accustomed to firing from a prone position at a target on a range, or who has little experience of any sort.

The sight of deer to those who are not accustomed to them can have the most astonishing consequences. In the 1950s when it was quite customary for roe deer to be shot as a matter of course when they emerged between the guns during a pheasant drive, it was surprising how many good game shots seemed incapable of killing them even at a range of ten or fifteen yards. During the eighteenth century when the American settlers often shot deer in similar drives, it was noted that some of the best wing shots from England seemed incapable of hitting deer driven past them in the same way.

Yet roe deer are easily enough killed with a shotgun at close range if the gun is swung freely and the shot is aimed behind their ears. The trouble is that too often the shooter becomes hypnotised by the size of the beast and fires into the brown, merely wounding it. The same thing on a smaller scale is often seen with hares. It is all a manifestation of buck fever. When anticipating a rocketing high pheasant the unexpected appearance of ground game sometimes flusters even very experienced guns and instead of swinging coolly and automatically as they would at a high bird, they fire wildly and either miss altogether or, worse still, wound it behind. It is for this reason that it is often argued that deer should never be shot with shotguns and as long the shooter is unsure of himself it is certainly better not to shoot. It is, however, entirely the man behind the gun, not the gun itself, that is at fault.

During a roughshoot on one occasion in the 1950s with three other guns I drove some pheasants up a glen to four other waiting guns and was pleased to hear a constant barrage of shots as we flushed a succession of birds forward. When we arrived at the other end it was only to find that the two guns on my side had each fired every shot we had heard at one unfortunate roe deer, which was lying very dead, over a fence midway between them. That these two experienced and good game shots had not even fired at one of the pheasants sent over them left me totally amazed at the time. Since then I have seen other examples of the same thing and I am no longer surprised at anything.

When a person is armed with a rifle, buck fever can have surprising effects. Faced with a deer the unfortunate sufferer may shut his eyes and pull the trigger, possibly firing several shots, none of which are likely to be anywhere near the deer. If he does hit the deer, it is likely to be the purest accident, for the victim in the grip of acute buck fever can be completely unaware of what is happening. After firing several shots into the blue it is quite possible that he is unable to recall even pulling the trigger. This may sound like an exaggeration, but anyone who has seen a bad case in action will recognise it.

Preparing to shoot

When actually preparing to take the shot, it is important to relax. The cheek should be firmly against the stock and the rifle should be held comfortably and firmly, but not gripped fiercely. The breath should be held and once the sights have been fixed on the point of aim the trigger should be gently squeezed, not pulled or jerked. Any haste, jerkiness, or wavering at this stage means a miss or, worse still, a wounded beast. If you feel the sights wavering, take a deep breath and hold still, then take aim again. Above all relax and avoid tension. Tenseness when taking aim is only one stage away from buck fever.

Whenever shooting with a rifle it is, of course, essential not to rest the barrel on a wall, a boulder, or anything similarly solid. The inevitable whip of the barrel which results will ensure that the shot goes wide of the target. The hand should interpose between any such solid object and the rifle barrel. If a rest is required in such circumstances make sure that a rolled-up hat, or waterproof, or some such soft material is interposed between the solid surface and the rifle barrel. Otherwise a miss is a certainty.

There are many ways of shooting with the rifle, but obviously it is best to use whenever possible the method to which you are personally accustomed, which gives you the best results. Confidence in any form of shooting is all-important. When shooting, many people like to carry a stick to use as a support. Well-seasoned hazel is a favourite, but any tough straight wood will do. If you are 6 feet (183 cm) tall then the stick should be at least 5 feet 10 inches (178 cm) to allow you to take a standing shot using it as a support. If taking a sitting or kneeling shot, you may also use the stick as a support. This can be very effective. It provides vertical, but not necessarily horizontal, support. In much the same way, using any tree or other natural support to lean against can also be a great help in steadying the aim.

Another considerable aid to shooting is using the correctly adjusted rifle sling to provide support. By slipping the elbow inside the sling it is possible to give the rifle barrel extra steadiness when required. Using this method it is possible to provide extra steadiness when lying on the ground, when sitting, kneeling or standing. With a little practice it is possible to slip the rifle off the shoulder and slide the elbow through the sling to give a steady stance and be ready to take a shot very quickly indeed. Again it is a question of what suits the individual best.

The stalking shot
It is, of course, hopeless to lay down any conditions about the actual position for the shot, since this is invariably dictated by the circumstances of the stalk itself. On the hill the final approach may at times be almost acrobatic. It may be necessary to crawl down a severe slope in order to get into position for a shot. In such circumstances it is generally inadvisable, to say the least, to try to crawl head first. The only way to crawl effectively and keep an eye on the deer at the same time may be on the back, feet first, so that it is necessary to take the shot by lying on the back and firing over the crossed ankles. This can provide a very stable platform and is also a quite surprisingly comfortable method of shooting once accus-

tomed to it and some people prefer it as a normal method of shooting, but practice is essential.

More obvious is the simple prone position, lying flat on the face with the elbows on the ground and the rifle to the shoulder in the widely accepted marksman's pose when shooting at a target, but it may be that this position has to be taken when climbing uphill so that the shot is almost taken standing upright and aiming directly uphill. In these circumstances the sling can be of great assistance, but a rolled-up cap or jacket may be useful if available as a rest for the barrel.

Whenever faced with taking a shot from a boulder, or a clump of heather or grass, always make sure of sliding round it, rather than leaning over the top. The deer will not so readily notice if the heather, grass, or boulder has an additional growth beside it, but a strange lump suddenly appearing on top of either will immediately alarm them. In woodland in the same way it is generally desirable to try to peer through vegetation, or stay close to a tree, rather than expose oneself more fully, but while merging with the background it is also essential to make sure of taking a shot clear of any possible deflection.

Very often in woodland a shot from around waist high through a gap in the trees may be the most suitable, or indeed the only way to take a shot free of intervening vegetation, or below branches and twigs. A kneeling shot is often advocated in such circumstances and if you like this method of shooting well and good. I find it somewhat unnatural and uncomfortable, possibly because I have a game leg. To my mind a sitting shot is then ideal. Indeed when shooting downhill the sitting position is often the best and only sensible method of taking a shot. Sitting with the legs crossed at the ankles, or feet planted apart, with the elbows tucked firmly into the inside of the thighs and the rifle sling giving added steadiness, this can be a very effective method of shooting. If the back can be set against a convenient tree or boulder, for added firmness, there are few better methods of shooting.

Taking the rifle from the stalker
On the hill there is sometimes a slightly tricky moment when it comes for the 'rifle' to take the rifle from the stalker. Some stalkers are so keen to put their 'rifle' in the best position that they tend to forget that he has been following patiently behind, freezing whenever the stalker froze, and following his every movement, possibly only aware of the soles of a pair of large studded boots a few feet

ahead of him and little else. This can often be the way of things and
the stalker meanwhile has the rifle. This is the normal practice,
since he naturally has no desire for someone behind him to be
carrying a loaded weapon. Usually the rifle is removed from the
sleeve and loaded at some distance from the deer but this is not
always possible. Then, when it comes to the hand-over, there is
sometimes something of a hiatus, with the need for some complicated acrobatics as the rifle is removed from its sleeve, loaded, then
handed to the 'rifle', with whispered instructions as to which beast
to shoot. All of this can be highly unsettling both to the 'rifle' and,
worse still, the deer. Many stalkers prefer to let the 'rifle' move into
the final position himself. Circumstances must generally dictate the
matter to a large extent. In any event it is probably advisable for the
'rifle' in the latter stages, if he can, to keep slightly above or to one
side of the stalker, so that he may more easily slide alongside him to
effect the transfer of the rifle comparatively simply and without
undue movement.

Placing the shot
Before shooting any deer it is important to know their anatomy intimately. If you have not seen a deer gralloched, or better still
skinned and butchered, you must rely on diagrams, but look at
these beforehand and study them well. If the beast chosen is broadside on there are several sound places to shoot. Before the day of
the flat trajectory people always used to advocate taking the sight
up the inside of the foreleg and squeezing the trigger when the
sights were aligned just behind the shoulder on the basic principle
that this is the largest vulnerable target area and a shot anywhere
here is likely to kill. It is up to everyone to make up his own mind as
to where he will take his shot, but I have some reservations about
this suggested method for several reasons. The heart and lungs are
situated behind the shoulder, with the heart at the lowest point
behind the leg. A shot in either of these will certainly kill the beast,
but it may then run as much as fifty or a hundred yards, or even further, after being shot.

   In dense woodland a beast which runs every ten or fifteen yards
may be hard enough to find and if it has run a hundred yards or
more it may well mean a lengthy and time-wasting search and
eventually having to go off for a dog to find the beast, even though
it is lying stone dead. There are even occasions when it may be lost
entirely or only found days later, by which time the venison is spoiled. On the hill a beast may run fifty yards or more clean over the

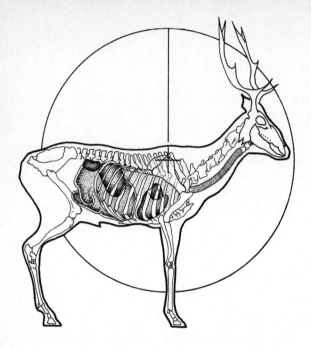

Skeletal anatomy showing desirable target area

edge of a precipice or onto a steep slope where it falls dead and rolls downhill for several hundred yards. In either case it will probably break every bone in its body, as well as its antlers, and the venison will be unfit to eat. Alternatively, should the aim be wavering slightly off target, or the trigger pulled too soon, this point of aim may result in a broken leg and a badly wounded beast which may be very hard to find.

There can be little doubt that the majority of deer are shot with a lung shot, simply because this is probably the largest target area and the easiest point of aim. It is, however, not necessarily the best shot to take. If the aim is a little shaky, or the beast is not broadside on, it is only too easy to end up with a gut-shot beast, which may be very hard to find and despatch.

Another shot, which is often advocated, is a neck shot, but again this appears to me to be unsound, since it may merely result in the bullet going through the windpipe and performing an unintentional tracheotomy, possibly causing a lingering death some days later. To my mind the best shot to take whenever possible is the spine shot just below the withers at the top of the shoulder. This should be easily enough taken with modern sights and rifles at a range of a hundred yards or so and if the bullet is slightly high it will mean a clean miss. If it is slightly low it will go through the shoulders and bring the beast down and it may then be killed cleanly with a second shot, if necessary. At the worst it may end up as a lung shot. Properly placed, this is a clean killing shot and the deer will fall stone dead on the spot.

The angle of shot
It seldom happens in practice that a beast is exactly broadside on and it is more often than not at a slight angle, even if this is not immediately obvious. If the deer is threequarters-on, looking away from you, as is often the case, a shot fired behind the shoulder will go through the lungs and probably exit through the far shoulder. If it is threequarters-on looking towards you, a shot behind the shoulder will go through lungs and liver, probably making an exit through the flank. If the deer is standing facing you, a shot placed where the neck joins the body will probably go through heart and lungs and may make a mess of the liver and intestines, but should kill it instantly. It is undesirable to take a shot when the deer is pointing directly away from you as the only way to kill it then is to aim for the anus, directly on the 'target', and such a shot is likely to damage one or both haunches, as well as possibly smashing the liver, heart, lungs and intestines.

In no circumstances should a head shot be attempted, however the deer may be placed. The danger is that you may simply shatter the jaw and should this happen and the deer then escape, it will certainly die miserably in agony, unable to eat or drink. There is no excuse for such a shot being taken, or attempted.

When firing steeply uphill it is important to aim your shot low in the body, thus a heart shot will go through the lungs and end up exiting through the top of the opposite shoulder. When firing steeply downhill it is equally important to aim slightly higher than might otherwise have been the case. Thus a shot behind the shoulder may go through lungs and heart, exiting below the brisket. When a shot is taken from immediately above the deer, as sometimes happens when shooting from a platform, it is advisable to shoot directly behind the withers, which should then go through spine, lungs and heart. This is a distinctly small target, much smaller than it may appear, and care must be taken not to miss, however close the deer may seem. It also probably means leaning awkwardly out of the high seat with the danger of being seen or alarming the deer. In such circumstances it will generally be worth waiting for a broadside shot, to make sure of it.

Shots at moving deer

Shots at deer on the move should in general never be taken unless a beast has been wounded and it is essential to try and kill it. Then it may be necessary to take a standing shot. There are basically two ways of doing this effectively. One is to swing through the moving beast with the telescopic sight, then pause and wait for the head to appear in the sight, when the trigger should be squeezed. This may result in the beast being hit on target and crumpling satisfactorily. Another and perhaps equally favoured method is to swing as described and squeeze the trigger while following the target and aiming at a suitable point. Swinging the rifle in this way, like a shot-gun, is quite effective for those used to it and if forced to take such a shot this is the method I personally prefer.

It is seldom that a deer in full flight will present a crossing shot broadside on, but when it does so the point of aim should be the shoulder as this will effectively bring the beast down with a heart or lung shot, or by immobilising the forelegs, cause it to somersault and break its neck. If the beast is quartering away from you the effective point of aim is behind the shoulder, when the bullet should enter heart or lungs emerging through the shoulder and killing the beast instantly in the same way. If it is going away from you do not aim at the back, head or neck, but take direct aim on the target. Although this may ruin one, or both haunches the bullet will enter the liver, heart and lungs and kill the beast instantly. The venison may have been spoiled but the beast will not have been allowed to escape to die slowly and miserably. To aim for the head in such circumstances is courting an almost certain miss as it is a much smaller mark and likely to be moving up and down.

It should be stressed that this advice is intended for those few occasions when it is essential to stop a wounded beast and there is no other alternative.

When a deer is lying down: or only partially seen

There are occasions when a deer is lying down and only a part of it can be seen. In such circumstances it is almost always best to wait, if possible until it rises. If all that can be seen are the antlers above a small rise, this may well be the only possible thing to do and a very weary business it can be, especially when you are being eaten alive by midges and flies, or steadily freezing into a block of ice. Thus it often happens that when the beast does decide to move you are incapable of reacting swiftly enough and fumble the safety catch and trigger, ending up with a hopeless miss at close range. Some people advocate whistling to attract the deer's attention, but this can result in alarming it so that it leaps to its feet and bolts at top speed. If you cannot, or will not, wait, it is probably best, as indicated earlier to try to imitate some natural call, such as a doe, or hind, or youngster in distress, to arouse the deer's curiosity.

In certain circumstances, especially during woodland stalking, when only a part of the beast can be seen, whether lying or standing, it may be essential to take a shot, since this may be the only chance of securing a beast it is desired to cull (e.g., a wounded beast). In such circumstances it is as well to know your deer's anatomy thoroughly. If only the forelegs and neck are visible a neck shot may be the answer. If only the forelegs and part of the body are to be seen a heart or spine shot may be possible. If only the hindquarters and part of the body are visible a spine shot again should suffice.

Once again, and it cannot be repeated too often, if only the head is visible, do not fire. Such a shot is almost always likely to wound rather than kill and to wound in such a way that the wretched beast dies a hideous death in agony. It should be stressed again, however, that it is always best at all times to have a deer in full view before shooting, even if this means waiting for a long time, or postponing the opportunity altogether for another day.

After the shot
The immediate reaction on firing a shot should be automatic. The gun should be re-loaded immediately without conscious thought, for if a second shot is required it is essential to take it as soon as possible. If there has been a miss for one reason or another, a second shot may often be taken before the deer is aware of what is happening and can locate the source of danger. Even if the beast is down and apparently dead it is essential to have another shot ready in case it was only stunned by a bullet shaving the spine or antlers, whereupon it may be up and away like a flash while the rifle is still unloaded.

Another reason for re-loading immediately after firing a shot is in case another deer, which it is desirable should be shot, appears on the scene. It happens surprisingly often that, after one deer has been shot successfully, some previously unnoticed beast which has been lying close at hand appears soon after the first beast drops, roused by the shot, but uncertain of the whereabouts of danger. It is always essential as a matter of routine to reload as soon as a shot has been fired.

Noting the reactions of the shot deer

While automatically reloading, the stalker should note the reactions of the deer at which he has shot. If it does not move or flinch, the shot has missed completely and another should be taken at once. If it arches its back and goes down, it has probably been gut-shot, too far back, and it will almost certainly get up again and move on. Another shot should be taken at once, if possible. If it leaps in the air and dashes off it has probably been shot in the heart or lungs and may run quite a distance before collapsing. In this case there will be no chance of a second shot, but the problem then may be finding the deer. If the deer falls down on the spot, it is advisable to advance smartly with the rifle at the ready, for it may just have been stunned and may get up and run off at full speed as you approach. In any event the stalker should mark the spot where the deer was shot and, leaving a marker such as his hat, or stick, on a bush at the spot where he took the shot, should advance as quickly as possible to where the beast was hit. Should no traces of the deer be visible and he subsequently decides he has made a mistake as to where it fell he can always return to his marker for a second look at the ground from where the shot was fired.

If the shot has been fired in the open and the deer runs off along with others, although it is uncertain whether it was hit or not, it is important to watch it carefully. If the deer go out of sight it is as well to count them if possible. Then if, say, five disappear from view and a few moments later only four are seen going over the next sky-line, the chances are the beast was hit and is down. It is anyway always worth keeping an eye on any beast that may have been shot for as long as possible in case it suddenly starts to stagger, or shows signs of weakening when facing a hill and veering off at a tangent. If there is any doubt, a close examination of the spot where it was standing when the shot was taken is necessary.

The approach to the shot deer

It is always advisable to approach a deer that has been shot at once, in case another shot has to be taken. If the deer is down an eye should be kept on it as the approach is made and the rifle should be ready for another shot if it is required, should the beast show any signs of attempting to rise. If it is obviously not dead, even though possibly mortally wounded, another shot should be taken at once. Above all, do not put the rifle down and take out your knife to gralloch the beast until you are sure it is absolutely dead.

On one occasion from the upper side of a glen I was able to watch a companion below me shoot a roebuck, put his rifle down, and run about twenty paces towards it with his knife in his hand before the buck rose to its feet and bounded off apparently unhurt, having only been stunned. On another occasion in an almost Laurel and Hardy sequence in almost identical circumstances from the upper side of a glen I saw a companion advance towards a roebuck which had been neck-shot. As he put his rifle down and took out his knife, the poor beast struggled to its feet and ran off for about fifty yards. By the time he had picked up his rifle again it had collapsed once more, apparently dead. Once more he ran fifty yards, put down his rifle, took out his knife and the roebuck once again struggled to its feet and ran a further fifty yards. To my total disbelief this performance was repeated no less than four times before he finally took a second shot and killed it.

When approaching any deer it is important always to make sure that it is in fact dead before taking out your knife. If there is no obvious wound it is not always possible to tell whether they are dead or merely stunned, as their eyes remain open. It is also as well to remember that a wounded beast can be dangerous. Even a roebuck can give a nasty wound if it kicks the knife in its death struggles and its feet and antlers are sharp. A red or sika stag's antlers are capable of inflicting a considerable injury. If the beast is still alive it is in the best interests of all concerned that a second bullet is put in its neck and a humane job made of it.

Safety first

As soon as it is certain the deer is dead and before gralloching it, the first essential is to unload the rifle. It is easy in the satisfaction of the moment to forget that the rifle is still loaded, but this must now be rectified at once. By all means leave the magazine full, but do not have a round in the chamber. Rifles have been known to go off on being dropped with the safety catch on, especially when fitted with a hair trigger. Accidents do happen, but they need the human element to cause them. Rifle safety cannot be overstressed.

7

After the Shot

MARKING, TRACKING, TRAILING AND THE DOG

Marking the shot

When stalking in woodland especially it is particularly important to mark the position where the deer is standing at the time of the shot; even in open ground it is desirable to do so. If the deer falls dead, nothing has been lost. If, however, when the shot has been taken, the deer then bounds off, but is thought to have been hit, it is a matter of considerable importance and urgency to be able to go to the correct place immediately to check whether there are any signs of the shot having taken effect.

It is thus important to mark some object such as a tree, bush or boulder close to where the deer was standing when the shot was fired. Leave a marker, such as your hat on a bush, at the place from which the shot was taken, but unless it was a particularly obvious place, do not take your eye off the spot where the deer was hit and then move as fast as possible to that point. As already noted, this enables you to return and take a second look at the ground from the exact position you fired the shot. Quite often, if you have inadvertently taken your eye off the spot, even for a moment or two, you will find that you have accidentally arrived at the wrong tree, bush or boulder. This is easily done, for it is not always easy to mark a spot exactly from a distance of 70–100 yards (64.7–92 m) or more.

Unfortunately, finding a deer in thick cover can be a very tricky business, even when it may have fallen stone dead quite close to where it was shot. A deer merges so closely with the background that very often it is hard to see even when you are quite close to it. It is thus essential to mark as closely as possible where it was standing when the shot was taken. It is also important to remember the reactions of deer to a shot. If it has leaped into the air, the chances are it was hit in the heart or lungs and it may be anywhere within a radius of a hundred yards, or sometimes a great deal more, especially during the rut when full of adrenalin. If it was completely missed, but a canny old beast which has been shot at previously, it may simply have departed at full speed at the sound of the shot, quite unharmed. This is one of the reasons it is very important to check for any traces of a wound at the site of the shot. It is, of course, equally important to find the right place if the deer fell down and immediately got up again and disappeared before a second shot could be taken. In this case it may have been gut-shot, or merely stunned for a second. In either case, you are aware it has been hit and it is important to look for all the available signs as to how seriously it has been wounded and so gauge how far it is likely to have gone. It is equally important to look for signs which will show you in which direction it has gone.

Signs to look for
If the deer was severely hit, there should be signs of blood as well as probably some traces of the deer's hairs to be found, either on the ground, or amongst nearby vegetation. Splashes of blood may be found at body height on nearby bushes. If the blood is thick and dark the deer is probably gut-shot and may travel a mile (1.6 km) or more. Alternatively it may have been hit in the liver, when it will probably lie down very soon and be reluctant or unable to move unless pressed. If the blood is frothy and orange-coloured, then it was hit in the lung and will probably die within a hundred yards (92 m) or so, with luck. If the blood is bright red, it probably means it has been hit in a leg, or the hindquarters. If there are pieces of bone in it then a leg may have been broken, but again it may travel a mile (1.6 km) or more. It is up to the stalker to retrieve his mistakes and it is unforgivable to leave a badly wounded beast to die without making every possible effort to find it.

Following the trail
When traces of a wound are found and duly assessed as serious, it is probably wisest to wait for up to half an hour or more to allow the beast to lie down and stiffen up. When pressed closely immediately after being shot, even a beast which is mortally hit seems to find a surge of adrenalin in the system which enables it to move off at speed and carry on for probably a much greater distance than would otherwise have been the case. Once signs of a blood trail have been found, if the stalker waits for half an hour or so, the chances are the beast will have stopped and, if badly hit, lain down. It will then stiffen quickly and gradually weaken with shock and loss of blood. Accordingly, after finding the blood traces, to fill in the time, it is worth sitting down and smoking a pipe, or going back and pacing the shot and retrieving the marker to fill in the time after finding the blood traces.

Once the blood from the shot has been found and examined and it has been decided that the time has come to follow up the trail, it is important to find the next signs of blood. By following the direction

the beast took it should be possible to find traces of blood, small splashes on the ground, or on leaves of bushes, within a few paces. If there are any slot marks to follow, assuming that the ground is

Muntjac in cover

soft enough to hold them, so much the better. The cleaves of the feet will probably be widely spread, indicating swift movement at the start, but if very soon the cleaves are close together the deer has not been able to move fast and this indicates a badly hit beast.

In any event a wounded deer will almost always take the easiest route from where it is hit. Unless closely pursued and full of adrenalin it will not head uphill, but will rather follow the contour of the hill, or turn downhill. It may be that it has turned for cover close at hand and its instinct is generally to head for the sanctuary of its bed. If the line of the wounded beast can be made out in the first ten yards or so it is usually easier to follow thereafter. It is the first part of any trail that is usually most difficult to find, so that time spent on this is usually well rewarded.

Once the line it has taken has been discovered it may be possible to follow the signs of blood on bushes, or on the tracks. Signs of hair on logs or similar obstacles, as well as bigger splashes of blood, may indicate that it has had to drag itself along and over them and this should mean that you are getting close to it. Be prepared therefore, with the rifle held at high port and ready to shoot, in case the deer with a last access of strength, starts to bolt again as you approach. In thick cover you may even be able to hear its movements or heavy breathing close at hand and it may then be worth rushing forward to the sound so that it exposes itself for another shot. In general, however, if a beast has been badly hit and is given around half an hour to settle down, the chances are that you will find it dead, although, as indicated, it is then not always easy to see, even when lying almost in full view.

The tendency is for the deer in its dying moments to drag itself into any form of cover available. It is also very likely to head for the nearest water, especially when gut-shot. Thus it is advisable at any stage in the trail to examine ditches, pools or streams, or patches of thick vegetation where the deer may have turned aside in its last moments for water or for cover.

If, after a lengthy search, you are still at a loss, make sure that you mark the trail as far as you have been able to take it. Then go back and find a dog, preferably one which has been trained to follow deer. Any ordinary gundog, even a terrier or collie, will probably be better than nothing. Most dogs when faced with the trail of a wounded deer will follow it keenly. A trained dog, of course, in such circumstances is a considerable asset. It rather surprises me that more has not been written on the subject of using dogs for finding wounded deer. It is on the whole comparatively simple to teach them what is required and once well trained such a dog is absolutely invaluable in finding a beast which has managed to vanish apparently without trace, even though known to be lying dead within quite a limited area.

The breed of dog

The breed of dog scarcely matters at all. Probably the best type of dog to use is one which is already well-trained as a gundog, simply because this will normally be easier to handle. In Germany the German Shorthaired Pointers and similar pointer-retriever breeds are trained for exactly this purpose. Thus they generally seem to take to the idea with very little training indeed, perhaps because it is inbred in them. On the other hand, collies and Jack Russells can be first-rate at the job. It is largely a question of introducing them to it correctly.

On one occasion when deer were driven to a friend he was unfortunate enough to wound a roebuck severely. We were aware that it had slipped into a patch of thick gorse in a steep-sided glen and had not come out. We also knew that it was either dead or dying, since we had found traces of blood indicating a badly shot beast leading in that general direction. After half an hour with little or no result he returned to his car and brought back his young golden retriever bitch, which had never seen a deer previously. When put on the trail she at once set off, following the line fast. It was extremely interesting to watch her from the top of the glen as she followed the scent along the contour of the hill through the gorse for nearly a hundred yards (92 m), then turned abruptly downhill and headed for the stream at the foot. There we could see her apparently attacking a gorse bush and at first we feared she was chasing a rabbit. On investigation, however, we found she was merely darting at the roebuck which was lying stone dead, having been shot through the lung and with a broken foreleg, but which had still managed to travel the best part of four hundred yards before finally expiring. Without a dog on that occasion it is extremely doubtful if we would have found the deer, although as a matter of principle I would probably have followed the banks of the stream and might in the end have been fortunate enough to find it.

Introduction and training
It is not a very difficult task to teach a dog that is already reasonably

well trained what is required of it in the way of tracking deer. The obvious first step is to shoot a deer and to lay a trail by dragging the body for some distance on a rope through cover, over a stream, if possible, and in general laying trail for the dog to follow. It is desirable, where feasible, to cover your own scent with that of the deer, so that the dog does not simply follow master's footsteps. In fact if you are hauling it on a rope this is more or less involuntary anyway, but it is preferable to try to avoid leaving any personal trail. Once the deer trail has been laid the deer should be left in a suitable position so that you can see it from a distance, or at least the place where it is lying. It is important then to walk directly away from the body of the deer and return to the start of the trail by a roundabout route, making sure that your scent is not blowing downwind to the dog when it is set on the trail. Even if the dog is accustomed to following wounded game it is probably as well not to make the first trail too difficult and it is probably better laid up-wind to make sure the dog is successful.

When you introduce the dog to the start of the trail there are two ways of setting about this. You can either turn the dog loose and encourage it to go off on the scent, or you can keep it on a lead and encourage it to follow the scent in this way. By using one of the extending leads made specifically for this purpose it is possible to give the dog freedom of movement and at the same time avoid entanglements with undergrowth. Some dogs, however, resent being on the lead and work better given free range. It is largely a matter of control and knowing your dog and trusting it. If the dog will work on the lead then it is simply a question of following it and encouraging it where you have made any breaks in the trail, if it requires assistance. An experienced gundog should have no difficulty in following the trail laid in this way or in leading you to the carcase of the deer, when, of course, it is most important to make a great fuss of him.

If you release the dog at the start the chances are that he will follow the trail at speed and leave you behind. Since at a later date you may want him to follow a wounded deer and if necessary hold him for you, this is not something to worry about unduly. It is an advantage, however, if in these circumstances you can lay the initial trail on a slightly uphill slope where you can watch the dog working it out, and encourage him where necessary while following him at speed. If you are going to let the dog go by himself and feel he may go too fast for you to follow easily, it is a simple enough matter to lay a winding trail in a half circle on a slope where he will

be visible to you and for you to cut across the radius while keeping
an eye on his progress.

The dog's reaction
The reaction of most Continental breeds of dog trained for the purpose is of two kinds. There is the dog that sits by the carcase and
bays – and until you have heard such a dog baying in full voice it is
difficult to appreciate how penetrating this can be. Even dogs
which are normally silent may well produce this extraordinary
sound when introduced to trailing deer. If they do this automatically, well and good. There is no need for any further action on your
part since it is quite easy to track down the sound from a distance of
half a mile or more and they will usually keep it up until their handler approaches them.

   The other reaction is for the dog to find the deer and then return
to its handler. The Germans equip such dogs with a length of
leather hanging from their collar known as a 'bringsel', which
literally may be interpreted as a 'retrieve'. The dog is trained on
finding the deer to take the 'bringsel' in its mouth and thus when
the dog returns with it in his mouth, the handler knows he has
found the deer. He then slips on the lead and encourages the dog to
take him to the deer. I have had both reactions in my dogs and
found that if they are allowed around ten minutes or a quarter of an
hour they usually return to the whistle and will then lead me to the
deer when encouraged to do so. I have not tried to teach them with
a 'bringsel' as this seems to me unnecessary if the dog has the right
instincts.

Possible reactions
Occasionally you may get the irritating animal, probably only part-
trained, which you have watched go direct to the deer and which
has returned to you directly after nosing the carcase, but which
shows no inclination to take you there. In such a case you should
slip on the lead and encourage the dog to follow the trail to the
deer, encouraging him all the way. Once you have reached it then
you must again make a fuss of the dog to show him that this was
what you wanted him to do, even if you have largely had to do it
yourself. In practice, even a dog which shows little inclination to
lead you to the carcase will almost certainly press forward in the last
few yards and this particular reaction should be made much of so
that he appreciates that this is what you wish him to do. Such a dog
might require several lessons, but it is not advisable to use the same
deer carcase more than once, for the dog is then well aware that the

whole affair is being staged for his benefit and is very likely to become bored with it, refusing to co-operate. For the same reason it is inadvisable to use the same piece of ground a second time.

If at the beginning it is felt that more than one lesson is going to be required to teach the dog, then it is advisable to start with a very simple trail of say only fifty yards (46 m) or so upwind. This can be followed with a longer trail upwind in a different area. Finally a trail downwind, with breaks, simulating a wounded deer crossing a stream, for instance, may then be attempted. On the whole, however, most dogs are so keen to follow up deer scent that it is rather a question of steadying them up than encouraging them to work it out.

When training the Continental breeds the initial reaction of the dog on arriving at the deer on the first laid trail will probably be sufficient to indicate which are the natural traits it has inherited, whether giving tongue and baying, or remaining mute, and it may be trained accordingly. Most ordinary retrievers, or other dogs, will work on the principle of finding the deer and returning to their master, although terriers yapping loudly may be almost as good as a trained dog baying to indicate where the dead beast lies. In many ways a dog that does give tongue is quite useful in this respect, but personally I prefer a dog which is mute, since a dog giving tongue throughout ground where deer are lying is very likely to make some of them desert the area and is anyway likely to make those remaining more alert and unsettled.

Other advantages of using a dog
In woodland stalking especially a dog can be very useful, if it is trained not to make a noise or to range, unless told to do so. I have found that most dogs are quickly aware on sight of the significant difference between a rifle and a shotgun. When the former is produced instead of the latter, after only a few outings they are aware of what to expect and an intelligent dog will react accordingly. On being taken out with the rifle it will not attempt to quarter the ground or hunt, but will remain at heel, showing considerable interest scenting the air and the ground as the still-hunt starts, but not moving from the heel position.

The first time I took one of my dogs on a stalking expedition and I went forward to a position overlooking a glen from where I hoped to see some deer, I made him sit and gave him the command to stay put. I then crawled forward for some twenty or thirty yards (18.5–27.5 m) to the edge of a glen, where I expected to find deer. I happened to glance back and found the dog, literally belly to the ground, crawling after me, eager not to be left behind. Thereafter I found that he could be extremely useful on such occasions as he clearly understood instinctively the difference between stalking deer and game shooting. When still-hunting he would literally crawl beside me, taking great care in his approach. He would also frequently point stiffly at apparently empty clearings and open spaces, whereupon I would always find there was a deer in the surrounding cover which would shortly make its presence known, either by appearing in full view, or partially coming into sight or, if it detected us first, making a noisy exit through the undergrowth. The advantage of having the dog's scenting powers aiding my own vision helped me many times to get a shot, which I might otherwise have never expected. The interesting point I noticed on such outings was that he rarely bothered about ordinary game, such as pheasants, or groundgame, but concentrated on deer. He was quite clearly able to differentiate between the different purpose of the shotgun and the rifle and the aims of the different outings.

Since then I have had many other dogs, most of which have taken naturally enough to stalking. Not many of them have been quite such a natural hunter and stalker as he was, but, with training, most of them have proved extremely useful in a number of ways. On the whole I do not think it is advisable to introduce them to stalking until they have been fully trained as gundogs for a season or two, since otherwise somewhat naturally they are liable to become confused as to what they are expected to do. Once any gundog has been trained as a useful retriever and pointer, however, or as a retriever alone, if it happens to be of a solely retrieving breed, then training it to come stalking can prove very useful. For instance they can be used to drive deer in a wood, as long as they have been taught not to give chase.

Once a dog understands what deer stalking is all about it can be a considerable asset. In woodland stalking especially, as indicated, the ability to scent the deer and thus sense their presence long before their handler is aware of them can prove of the greatest assistance. If the handler can trust his dog to warn him of the presence of deer in an area he is thus able to take much greater care stalking when he knows deer are nearby and can afford to freeze for some time, waiting for them to appear before he moves. Another point in the dog's favour is that he has the benefit of looking through undergrowth at the same level as the deer. He can sometimes see, as well as scent, the deer long before his master is aware

of them and if he gives warning by stiffening silently on point, regardless of his breed, this is clearly an added advantage.

The scent of deer

Most deer have a fairly strong scent at any time, but especially
during the rut it can become very strong indeed. Anyone who has
smelt a fallow buck in the rut will appreciate that billy goats are not
the only males that smell strongly. Even a human, when out stalking, may often have smelt deer. The smell of a roebuck during the
rut can be almost as rank as a fox and not dissimilar. It is not uncommon for a stalker to get a whiff of deer scent from time to time when
the wind is right. It is certainly a strong scent and a good dog
should be able to follow it with comparative ease. Although fawns
and calves are supposed not to have any scent in the early stages, I
do not personally believe this to be the case as I have frequently had
my own dogs point a comparatively new-born fawn lying in cover.
On one occasion when I was out at dawn I found a large blood trail
in the road and hairs indicating that a roe had been hit. My dog
quickly led me to the place where a doe badly hit by a car had
dragged itself with a broken spine into the cover by the roadside.
Seeing that it was an in-milk doe I set the dog to quarter the ground
and within a matter of a quarter of a mile (406 m) had pointed two
very young fawns, not much more than a day or two old. Sadly,
despite our efforts to rear them, neither of them survived more than
a few days. (For the benefit of those who may be in the same position and wish to rear an abandoned fawn, or calf, powdered milk
fed in very small quantities at about four-hour intervals seems to be
the best hope for them. It is important, however, not to feed them
too much.)

Failure to find the deer

If, despite all your efforts, you fail to find a deer that you are con-
vinced is wounded it is advisable to spread the word around
amongst foresters, farm labourers and others who may possibly see
the beast. If there is any possibility of it having gone onto neighbouring ground it is also, of course, desirable to warn your neighbour to keep an eye open for it. Thereafter, at dusk and dawn, you
should yourself be alert for any beast which shows signs of having
been wounded. It is in fact surprising how badly a deer may seem
to be hit and yet display amazing recuperative powers. If, for
instance, a bullet has fragmented and only a portion wounds the
deer, this may cause a considerable blood trail which just peters out

in the end. The beast itself may recover without any trouble. Even when badly shot they may well recover. Such injuries as broken legs may well knit in course of time and will not prevent such a beast from either mating or having young. The sometimes horrific injuries deer incur when hit by cars are quite often found to be more than partially healed at a later date when a deer is shot. In principle, however, if a deer is seen to be suffering from an obvious injury, such as trailing a broken leg or limping badly, it should be stalked and culled whenever possible. The same, of course, holds good of any deer which has not cast its coat, is coughing badly, or otherwise shows signs of being sick. No ailing beast should be left to die, whether of injury or illness, if it can be avoided.

It is probable, however, that any stalker of experience will have encountered beasts, sometimes with limbs missing or with traces of very serious injuries, which have somehow recovered and continued to lead a more or less normal existence. Deer may be found from time to time which have caught a hind leg in the top wire of a fence which has then twisted over and caught them, as in a wire snare. Usually such beasts are condemned to a lingering death of starvation and their corpses are to be found, mute evidence of a miserable end. On the other hand, sometimes the leg will be broken at the joint of the pastern and if the beast is a heavy one it may jerk its remaining limb free. I have shot at least two large roebucks in fine trim except for one hind leg missing at the pastern joint, but with a barely perceptible lameness and clearly able to lead a normal life in every way.

Unfortunately, a three-legged deer can move amazingly well, even though a foreleg or a hind leg is dangling. It is for this reason that I am strongly against hair triggers and the principle of taking a shot by following up the line of the foreleg. Unintentional pressure in such circumstances can only too easily result in a broken leg and a beast left to die in agony, or at best to survive as a cripple after a lengthy period of lying up.

Of course, regardless of how careful anyone may be, there are those occasions when a shot, for one reason or another, fails to kill and merely wounds a deer. A deer may move unexpectedly at the moment of squeezing the trigger: the telescopic sights may have received an unnoticed jolt and have gone out of alignment: an unseen twig may have deflected the bullet: all these and many more reasons may cause a deer to be accidentally wounded. Whatever the reason, and they are legion, it is always incumbent on the person responsible to find that deer if it is humanly possible. If it is not humanly possible then a dog should be used. If a good dog cannot find the deer the chances are that it was not as badly wounded as was at first thought. At least the stalker will have done everything he can to ensure that the beast has not died a lingering death through any lack of effort on his part. That is the duty of anyone stalking. If, for any reason whatever, and it is accepted that it may well not be his fault, the stalker has failed to make a clean kill, he must still try to ensure that no wounded deer is left to suffer in misery.

8

When the Deer has been Shot

Dealing with the carcase

Once the deer has been found and is undeniably dead, the next stage is dealing with the carcase. If a deer is not properly bled before *rigor mortis* sets in the venison may be very nearly uneatable. If it is only partially bled the venison will not taste as good as it would if the arteries were correctly emptied while the blood is still warm enough to flow freely. It does not take long, in freezing weather especially, for the blood to coagulate, so the sooner the beast is bled the better, if you are going to eat the venison yourself.

Dealing with the carcase of the deer correctly from the gralloch, the Gaelic word for removing the intestines now in general use, to skinning and jointing the beast, is a skilled job, which requires knowledge of anatomy and experience. On the hill the professional stalker will take charge of this as a matter of course. In woodland stalking initially it is very advisable for the beginner to have someone experienced standing by to demonstrate what to do and how to do it. The novice should watch carefully at each stage and only attempt it initially with skilled guidance on hand, for there is a great deal more to the task than might at first appear to be the case. Almost anyone can butcher a deer, but performing the task of skinning and jointing the carcase neatly, quickly and without fuss or mess is another matter. It requires considerable experience and practice from the first stages in the field to the last stages in the larder.

Bleeding
The first step is to bleed the carcase. The ideal is to remove as much blood from the arteries as possible before it starts to coagulate. The first step is to lay the body on a slope with the head slightly downhill and pulled backwards so that the throat and chest are exposed. Then insert a sharp knife with a blade 4–5 inches (10–12.5 cm) long in the base of the neck where it joins the body. Thrust the blade in and turn it, thus cutting the main arteries entering the heart; this will release most of the blood. In order to ensure that as much of the blood as possible is pumped out of the body it is advisable to work the legs, starting with the hind legs, by bending them vigorously a

few times. When the blood flow eases to a trickle the job is complete. There should then be a considerable pool of blood soaking into the ground. Of course, if the bullet has penetrated the lungs or heart, the carcase may be full of blood, which may need to be emptied out when the intestines have been removed.

The gralloch

The next stage is to remove the intestines. The carcase should now be reversed, with the head uphill. Start by pinching a fold of the skin over the base of the stomach and making a slit transversely across it. Then insert a hooked finger in the hole and run the knife up the stomach wall towards the chest cavity, keeping it clear of the intestines right up to the rib cage. The cut can then be extended down to the anal passage. It is then advisable to cut carefully round the anus and ease the contents inwards. The sheath and scrotum should also be cut round at the same time. One of the main objects of these preparations is in order to remove the bladder and its contents whole along with the rest of the intestines, without it bursting inside the carcase and tainting the meat.

The next stage is to widen the hole cut for the bleeding and reach in and pull out and cut out the 'thropple' (i.e., trachea and oesophagus). Everything is then free of its attachments and the entire stomach and intestines can be eased out onto the ground, if necessary on larger beasts by reaching in and hauling with both hands. If you wish to remove the liver, lungs and heart at this stage your hands are likely to become even bloodier, but a little dry earth and grass can soon remove the traces. On the hill there is usually a burn handy. You should be carrying two plastic bags into which these can be placed. The body cavity may then be left propped open to allow for quick cooling, unless the flies are very bad.

Hocking and hanging the carcase

Another method, only really suitable in woodland stalking is to hock and hang the carcase for bleeding and gralloching. If one hind leg is slit above the hock and the other is thrust through it this provides a natural loop. The hocked carcase can then be hung from the branch of any suitable tree. Where the ground is flat this certainly makes the bleeding and gralloching somewhat simpler. A lot depends on the circumstances, since while it is easy enough to deal with a roe or lesser deer in this manner, anything larger requires two to handle it comfortably. On the whole there is really not much gained by this method if there is a suitable piece of sloping ground at hand.

In either case it is advisable to have a trowel or spade handy, if possible, to dig a hole for the intestines. It is not really desirable to leave them in the open as encouragement for foxes and carrion eaters such as crows or gulls. On the hill this may be a refinement, but if the transport can reach the scene there is no reason why a spade should not be carried for the purpose. Leaving the gralloch around not only encourages carrion eaters; it is liable to make deer shun the area for some time.

The haul
Once the gralloching has been completed it is merely a question of transporting the carcase to the larder. This is often a great deal easier said than done. If the deer happens to have been shot conveniently within easy reach of home it may well be, especially with an easily carried carcase such as that of a roe, that the entire body is carried back to be duly gralloched with ease in the precincts of the larder. This has the advantage that there is less likelihood of blood being spread over one's hands or person. Carrying a gralloched roe can often result in smears of blood on the clothes, even when equipped with all the requisite gear. A roe is usually best carried in a waterproof/bloodproof washable rucksack strapped on the back. A roe can also be very readily carried, if the legs are hocked and the forelegs slipped through the hindlegs to provide a suitcase effect. I have quite often carried two roe for a mile or more, balancing each other in this way with a rope over the shoulders to distribute the weight evenly. It gets a little tedious, but so does any load amounting to 75–90 pounds (32–40 kg) or thereabouts. Any lengthy haul becomes tiring after a while, however fit one may be.

If there are two of you to haul a roe, the use of a stick slipped through the hocked legs in the time-honoured fashion for transporting game is probably the best method, unless you prefer to take it in turns to carry it. The only alternative is to take an end each and this can often prove awkward on a long haul, involving frequent changes of ends.

Hauling a red deer, a fallow, or sika, which may weigh anything from 10–11 stone (63–70 kg) up to as much as 17 stone (108 kg) or even more, is another matter altogether and can be a very much more taxing business. A great deal depends on the ground and the distance over which the carcase has to be hauled. In most places, fortunately, motorised transport of one sort or another, four-wheeled or tracked, can usually be expected to reach you. Failing that, in most deer forests a deer pony may be available. Yet there are occasions which any regular stalker will have encountered when even the pony cannot get near you because of bottomless bogs, or similar obstacles, or else even a pony is not available. Even in woodland stalking a haul of some distance may be required to get a beast to where it can be reached by wheeled transport.

Even 3-400 yards (276–369 m) hauling a 15–16 stone (95–102 kg) stag over various obstacles, especially those deep forestry drains, can be a very taxing business. I have had more occasions to haul deer long distances than I dare to remember, but one episode when the stalker and I had to haul a 17 stone (108 kg) stag up two 15 foot (4.5 m) waterfalls still remains vividly in my memory! After some twenty minutes of the start of that day I was wet through. By the end of it, with a ten-pointer grassed, I was soaked to the skin. As I hauled that carcase up the waterfalls and felt icy water pouring down my neck and out of my breeks my only feeling was that it was quite a refreshing change. However, everything comes to an end and when you are back at the lodge and the deer is hung in the larder it all suddenly seems worthwhile.

For short hauls with two people the simplest method is probably to take an antler apiece and haul away. Going downhill is comparatively easy, but care must be taken that the beast does not catch up with you and run you down. It is usually desirable to move downhill at an angle, but again it is important not to let the carcase take charge and run away with you. On the flat, when hauling it through peat hags or over obstacles such as waterfalls, the hauling is pure muscle-power and weight. If a long haul has to be done it is better to use a rope. This should be lashed round the base of the antlers to prevent them snagging the ground as far as possible. Another method is to cut off the head and legs and insert the rope through a hole cut in the tough neck skin. With two people, two ropes attached to sticks or toggles sometimes makes for easier hauling. It can still be a major exercise when it comes to obstacles such as bogs, peat hags, or waterfalls.

If you are faced with a mile or two (1.5–3 km) of real rough country covered in bogs or deep plough, it may be that you have to resort to the old poacher's trick of cutting the carcase in two, by severing the spine behind the rib cage. The haunches can then be carried on the back with the legs over the shoulders like the handles of a wheelbarrow. This is still a considerable weight to carry over rough going, but in some circumstances, as for instance if it is snow-ing heavily, it may be the only possible way to save the greater part of the venison.

Every deer forest seems to have its own methods of transporting deer. In some it is accomplished by boats over a loch and this can also sometimes be a wet business hauling the deer on board. In other forests sledges may be used which are left at recognised places for use when necessary. A similar less expensive, but quite convenient, method sometimes used is to leave pieces of corrugated metal bent up at the front to act in the same way as an aid to hauling a stag over the rough ground. This is quite a useful idea as deer can be hauled on them comparatively easily, whereas hauling them by sheer muscle-power is always exhausting, especially if the head is left in position, as the antlers will tend to catch from time to time on tussocks of heather and similar obstacles, particularly when it is getting dark.

In the larder

When the deer is in the larder it should be hung head upwards, with a hook through the lower jaw. If they have not already been removed, the four legs should be cut off at the knee and hock joints. The carcase should then be hung for a suitable period. In summer, in hot weather, this may be no more than a day or so. (The larder, needless to say, must be fly-proof.) In the winter it may be as much as a week. Then it is time to skin and butcher it. The first requirement for this is a sharp knife and preferably a good butcher's saw.

Skinning the deer

This is something that can take from five to ten minutes up to two hours depending on the experience of the skinner, also on how particular you are as to removing it in one piece to retain as a floor or chair covering. A deerskin can, of course, be quite an attractive asset in this way. Once it starts to moult, as in the end it will, it can be decidedly tiresome. The same, of course, holds true of tiger skins and other trophies of the chase in a greater or lesser degree. No doubt ancient man, who after all clothed himself in skins, decided each year that it was advisable to invest in a new suit when he found his old one beginning to moult. Deerskins properly skinned and prepared will, admittedly, last a number of years before they begin to wear badly, but no skin, however well cured, will last for more than a decade or so before shedding hairs, or showing signs of wear. A lot, of course, depends on the state of the skin in the first place. If the deer was moulting, or changing coat, it will almost certainly be a hopeless task and not worth trying to preserve the skin.

While offering a method of skinning, which I have often used, I would be the first to admit that there are many others. Indeed, most serious stalkers have probably developed their own methods over the years. Skinning tends to be a highly individual business and, as indicated, a great deal depends on whether you wish to preserve the skin or not.

Although it is perfectly possible to skin a carcase on the ground it is advisable to have a sheet of canvas underneath to keep it clean. It is preferable to skin it when it is hanging. Assuming that the deer has already been jointed at the knees and hocks the first incision should be made starting from the right or left foreleg, from the joint under the skin to the brisket and then to the throat. From here downwards it is necessary to ease the knife under the skin on the same side where the cut has been made for the gralloch down to the hindleg. When the skin and the body have been separated throughout from the foreleg and neck down to the hindleg, slit the skin to the joint of the hindleg. By then you should have an area of skin raised from the body almost completely down one side.

Continuing back down the hindleg you now separate the skin from the flesh on the lower side of the hind leg and progress back to the body. It is then necessary to make a cut up the hind leg on the other side and finally reverse the procedure, removing the skin from the body on the other side of the carcase. Once you have returned to the starting point the skin and body should be separated all round. Thereafter it is merely a question of pushing, pulling, or punching the skin and body apart, using the knife where it is felt necessary, although after the initial separation all round the knife should not be really needed. With a young deer the process is naturally much easier than with an old deer.

On the whole, the skinning of a beast is more reminiscent of punching a punchbag, or hauling on a tarpaulin, than a gentle operation. It is much more a physical exercise than a neat piece of surgical skill. One point worth bearing in mind is that when you come to the place where the bullet entered or exited you may find bones, jagged ribs, or even fragments of bullet, which can cut you or blunt your knife if you are not careful in these areas.

Jointing the carcase
When the carcase has been divested of its skin, the next stage is jointing it in the most satisfactory manner. The jointing, or butcher-

ing of any beast varies remarkably from area to area and country to country. Just as much as skinning, it is essentially a local custom varying from place to place. Thus I can only put forward the way in which I personally joint a carcase. It may well be that you have an entirely different and much preferred local method. In any event it is always worth discussing it with your local butcher. He is bound to have some useful tips and if you are friendly with him he can be very helpful. For instance, a large red deer haunch makes a massive joint, far too large for most people. It is extremely helpful if you can persuade your butcher to cut it into sections with his bandsaw, making in effect large steaks with a bone in the centre. Cleaning a bandsaw is quite a tiresome job, so it is as well to find out when he is using it anyway and then asking him to take on any such jobs for you. In return for a steak or two, or at most a nominal charge, most butchers will be happy to oblige a customer in this way.

When it comes to jointing the meat, I prefer to start by removing the forelegs, which is simply a question of slicing down from behind the shoulder-blade. There are no connecting bones or joints and the whole foreleg comes away very easily with the aid of a knife. If you like, you can then remove the flesh and roll the meat off the bone, but be warned that this is a skilled and tedious operation and barely worth it.

Perhaps the best meat on the deer is to be found on each side of the spine, above and below the spinal column, running from the haunch right up to the neck. On a fat beast the meat trimmed close to the spine with a sharp knife can produce some very excellent steaks. The underside especially can be the best meat on any beast.

The neck is duly sawn off with the hand saw. It may then be sawn into four or five sections, which make a good casserole. The spinal column may then be sawn through above the haunches and all the remaining pieces may be put in the stock-pot to provide soup. This may sound rather drastic, but there really is not much on the ribs of a deer and after the meat has been removed from the spine all that remains is only suitable for soup. I know that some people may be shocked by this suggestion since they like making venison cutlets and similar small joints. This is purely a matter of choice and if you prefer it that way, by all means butcher your carcase accordingly.

The final stage is to deal with the haunches by separating them with the saw down the spine. This leaves each haunch with the pelvic bones attached. It is desirable to cut the pelvic bones and spinal column out, without losing too much meat in the process. The haunch should then be trimmed and the leg bone chopped down to make it a compact size for the oven. Each is then duly packed and labelled in a freezer bag and that is two prime pieces of meat in the deep freeze. The pelvic bones and the back end of the spine with any remaining meat adhering to them are really only suitable for soup.

Cooking

If the deer has been properly bled and the beast is a young one, the meat should be treated much the same as any other prime meat. It is hard to improve on grilled steaks of venison.

Grilled steaks
Sprinkle with a little olive oil and pepper and some fresh herbs to taste before grilling. Cut the steaks ½–¾ inches (1.5 cm) thick. Anoint with olive oil, sprinkle on the pepper and herbs and leave to soak for a couple of hours. Grill them for 3–4 minutes on both sides and serve with a suitable sauce and wine.

Haunch of venison in beer, or cider
Ingredients:
2 lb (0.9 kg) haunch of venison
One tablespoon olive oil
One large onion
½ pint (250 ml) of beer, or cider.
½ pint (250 ml) venison stock, or consommé
1 crushed clove of garlic
1 tablespoon brown sugar
bouquet garni
black pepper
1 tablespoon flour
Slice the onion finely then brown the haunch in a casserole dish in the oil on top of the onion. Add the beer or cider, the stock, crushed garlic, bouquet garni and sugar and leave in a covered casserole dish in a moderate oven for 1–1½ hours, basting occasionally.
   Before dishing the meat, a coating of a tablespoon of cream and a teaspoon of mustard may be added. Leave in the oven while taking off the fat for gravy. Mix the fat with the flour in a pan, add this to the gravy and bring to the boil. Then serve together.
   Note: Most older venison will be vastly improved if left to soak in a marinade for up to 24 hours before cooking.

Curing the skin

If you want a really professional job done on a skin, the best advice is to send it to a professional. Sprinkle it liberally with salt and send it to a tannery, if you know of one, or to a taxidermist. Alternatively, you may try sprinkling the skin with baking soda or alum, obtainable from any chemist. First the skin should be pegged out tightly on a board and a pumice stone applied to remove most of the fatty tissue. Then baking soda and alum should be applied liberally and the result should be left to dry. After a few days further treatment may be given with a pumice stone and further application of alum and soda. After about six weeks the skin should be sufficiently cured to make a rug.

Preserving the head

For those who wish to preserve the whole deer-head as a trophy it is important to preserve the antlers and the skin as far down the neck as possible, at least from above the shoulders. By all means work back from there and sever the neck several inches higher, but the taxidermist always likes to have as much free skin as possible to mount the trophy in a natural manner.

Preserving the antlers

If it is only desired to preserve the antlers it is much easier. A saw will be required and the initial cut made about 3 inches (7.5 cm) behind the antlers and the cut continued to the jaw line. This part of the head should then be skinned and the surplus flesh removed. It should next be boiled in a large saucepan filled with bleach and water, keeping the antlers from the coronet upwards clear of the water until the surplus flesh has been boiled away. It can then be trimmed to the required shape to mount on a plaque to hang on the wall as a trophy.

Trophy measurement

There are those who like trophies and those who do not. To cull when necessary is one thing, or to shoot for meat, but not for glorification. Yet I know otherwise apparently intelligent people who will solemnly hack the head off every beast they shoot and preserve the antlers whether good, bad, or indifferent. I can see the point of keeping perhaps one particularly outstanding head, or a head which reminds one of an epic stalk, or some such memories. Two, or even three, might be forgiven. I can understand also the man who likes unusual heads, which might otherwise be condemned as rubbish. Yet it seems to me that very often people who collect trophies, like other forms of collecting, simply do not know when to stop. There are those who will keep every head they shoot and even ones they have not shot and end up with them hung around outhouses or garages. They may even end up calling this collection a museum and in truly large collections it may even end up being one, but such Golgothas really should be something of the past.

One has only to visit the Duke of Fife's amazing mausoleum outside and inside the hall at Mar Lodge, on upper Deeside, to see where this can lead. It seems to me that with the advent of photography there can be no longer any excuse for this sort of collection. If a permanent record is required then all necessary measurements and details of where and when shot and by whom can be included on the page of an album facing a colour photograph. That is surely all anyone requires. Only exceptional fish are destined to end in glass coffins and most fishermen have to be content with pictorial records of their epic bags, so why not the deer stalker as well? The only logical reason for keeping such heads, apart from personal gratification, is as a record of the type of head shot in a certain area for comparison, possibly, with other heads at a later date in that or other areas. This is a perfectly reasonable requirement which can be adequately fulfilled by a photographic record.

Only a very few outstanding and exceptional heads merit preservation. In most of today's houses there is also little enough room for them. They are regarded by most people with justice as dust-gathering relics. For those who both like and want them, however, nothing said, or written, is likely to deter them from decorating their walls with what are euphemistically and romantically termed 'trophies of the chase', but could be more accurately described as archaic by-products of the modern technological revolution in the firearms industry.

However, each to his own taste. If you think you have shot a record head, whether red, fallow, roe or even muntjac and wish to have it recorded you will anyway have to submit it for examination and accurate measurement. There seems to me absolutely no point therefore in laying out the extraordinarily complex details of measurement whereby heads are measured under the International system. The very simple British system will at least let you know whether you have a head of proportions worth submitting for the much more involved International method.

To measure red deer heads under this British method the procedure is given by Frank Wallace in his book *British Deer Heads*, published by Country Life in 1913.

The *length of horn* (sic) is measured: from the bottom edge of the burr (or coronet) to the highest tip point, following the outside curve of the horn.

The *Beam (circumference)* measured between bay(bez) and tray (trez), that is, between the second and third points: where the bay is absent, between the brow and tray.

The *inside span*: the greatest width between the main beams taken in a straight line.

Hence the overall measurements are given both right and left antlers: number of tines: length of tines: beam: followed by the inside span. The average length of antlers of a highland red stag is between 31–34 inches (78–86 cm). Length in itself, however, is not all-important. Anything over this with at least twelve points and notable beam measurements ought to be worth measuring under the International scale for those who are keen on records.

For the measurement of fallow deer heads the length is again not all-important. The measurement is taken from the outside bottom edge of the burr following the curvature across the lowest depression between the tines of the upper edge of the palmation. The width of the palmation is measured at the point of the deepest depression between the tines and at approximately right-angles to the top edge. The total measurements by the British method therefore are the length, right and left; the beam, right and left; the width of the palmation; the tines and the inside span.

Roe antlers are measured from the outside lower edge of the burr up to the tip of the upper tine. The measurements by the British system are therefore, the length, right and left antlers; the circumference of the coronet, right and left; the span from tip to tip, or at the broadest inside point if the tips turn inwards. Anything over 9 inches (23 cm) with notable pearling is probably worth at least measuring more accurately. For International measurement of roe antlers a method of scoring by volume displacement in water is used as well as overall weight.

Muntjac are measured by the length of the main beam, the circumference of the coronet, the length of the brow tine and the inside span. Any length of 9 inches (23 cm) is more or less bound to qualify for a bronze medal and is worth checking, if so desired.

Mounting a head
It is really not a very difficult task to mount a head. A suitably sized

shield can be readily enough made if you are handy with a saw. An
effective enough backing can be made by simply sawing a suitable-
size log into rounds. The head itself can be secured by a couple of
screws through the orbital artery holes. The whole thing is so
simple that it is understandable why it becomes a vice with some
people. I still strongly recommend keeping the number of heads
preserved to a minimum, for apart from anything else this will
always give you a standard to maintain.

Legal addendum

Legal points to note
It is an offence to kill deer, or attempt to do so, during the close
seasons, except if an 'authorised person', i.e.:

1 the occupier of the land on which the action is taken;
2 any member of the occupier's household acting with their written authority;
3 any person in the occupier's employ, so acting;
4 any person with the right to take or kill deer on the land;
5 any person with the written authority of 4 above.

Such 'authorised persons' may claim:

a. that the deer was injured, or diseased, and the action taken was
to prevent suffering;
b. that it was done in pursuance of a Ministry requirement under
Section 98 of the 1947 Agriculture Act: i.e., when deer are causing damage the Minister may require them to be shot;
c. if there was good reason for believing the deer were causing
damage to crops, timber or fruit and that further serious damage
was likely to occur.

It is an offence to kill deer at night except where one of the defences
1 and 2 above is available.

Deer poaching
By the Deer Act of 1980 it is an offence:

1 To enter land in search or pursuit of any deer with the intention
of killing or injuring it.
2 While on any land;
   i. intentionally to kill or injure, or attempt to kill or injure, any
   deer.

ii. to search for or pursue deer with the intention of killing or injuring it;

iii. to remove the carcase of any deer.

Defences to these acts are if the person committing them:

a. has the consent of the owner or occupier of the land;

b. has lawful authority;

c. believes that he would have the consent of the owner or occupier of the land if the owner or occupier knew of the act and the circumstances of it;

d. believes that he has other lawful authority.

If an authorised person suspects with reasonable cause that another person is committing, or has committed, any of these offences on any land, he may require that person to give his full name and address and to leave the land at once; failure to do this is an offence.

The 1980 Act also regulates the sale of venison and requires licensed game dealers to keep records of their sales.

A Glossary of terms used in Deer Stalking

(With some Ancillary Sporting and Forestry Terms)

Albino: of deer: absence of pigment in the skin and hair with pink eyes: rare in deer

Anointing post: of deer: a tree, or stump, with a part of the trunk worn smooth and oily as a result of deer depositing gland secretion on it

Antlers: of deer: a bony outgrowth on the head of males: they are described as carrying antlers not horns

Bald-faced: of deer: with a white blaze covering its face

Bark: of roe and muntjac: distinctive sound made by both species: red deer are also known to bark on occasions

Barking: of trees: the removal of bark from a tree by a deer's teeth

Bay: of a stag's antlers: the second tine, or point

Beam: of antlers: the main stem

Beat: of forest: area under one forester

Beating up: of forestry: replacing damaged, or failed trees

Bed: of roe: when retiring to rest

Black: of a stag: when it has been rolling in a peat bog

Block: of a forestry plantation: an area of forestry generally delineated by broad rides or fire-breaks: *see Ride*

Blue hind: on the hill: a hind which has not bred in the previous season: so called because of colouring; *see also Yeld*

Brash: of forestry: to remove the lower branches of a plantation at the thicket stage to prevent choking and allow free growth: *see Thicket*

Brocket: of male red deer: a second year beast, sometimes used to refer to a third year beast as well

Brow: of an antler: the lower point, also sometimes known as the first antler

Browse: of a deer: when eating foliage: *see Feed*

Browse line: the level up to which a deer has eaten the foliage on trees and bushes, from which the size, age and type of deer may be assessed

Buck: correct term for male roe, fallow, muntjac or Chinese water deer

Bunch: of hinds: (colloq.) a group

Burr: the rough outer edge of the coronet: *see Coronet*

Butcher's weight: of deer: the weight of the skinned and cleaned carcase minus head and feet with only the kidneys and liver left in place

Button(s): of stag or buck: the first sign of growth of new antlers: hence: thrust out their buttons: of a deer when starting to develop new antlers

Button-head: of young roebuck with small first-year antlers

Cabers: a switch head, of only two points, or at most four: *see Switch*

Calf: young of red, or sika, deer

Calling: of deer: method of bringing deer within range of rifle by imitating call: of roe, the call of the doe to attract the buck: of red, the call of the stag, to attract either sex

Canopy: of woodland: where crowns of forest trees meet overhead forming continuous cover

Cannon bone: of deer or horse: the long bone of lower leg: *see Metacarpal/ Metatarsal*

Cast: of antlers: when shed by male deer

Catch up: of deer: to trap deer for removal to another area, for injection, or examination, identification, etc

Challenge: of a stag in rut: when roaring at a rival

Clean: of antlers: when the velvet has dried up and been worn off

Clean: of a deer's weight: after the lungs, stomach and intestines have been removed: the liver, heart and kidneys, being edible, are usually included, but customs vary

Cleave: of deer: the toe: the two cleaves make a cloven foot common to deer and most ruminants (in tracking deer the spread between the cleaves indicates speed as size indicates age and sex)

Coat: of deer: commonly used to describe skin

Close-season: of deer: the months of the year when it is illegal to shoot, or hunt deer

Compartment: of forestry; area used for purposes of management: usually about 20–30 acres (8–12 ha.)

Coppice: of hardwoods only: a crop growing from the roots of the previous crop

Core area: naturalist's term used for the area of its home range an animal frequents

Coronet: of the antler: the base above the pedicle

Corrie: in highlands: cleft, gulley or bowl in hills where deer may find shelter and or grazing

Couple: of animals: to mate

Cover: of animals: to mate

Cover: may be used of any foliage, or undergrowth, sufficient to provide a deer or other quarry with shelter or concealment

Creep: of deer: a hole under wire, fence, hedge or similar obstruction where deer have chosen to go under rather than over

Cromie: of red deer antlers: stunted and goat-like: said to be not uncommon on Jura

Crotties, or Croties: of roe and fallow deer: becoming obs: piles of droppings

Crown: of red deer antlers: if the three topmost points are in the shape of a crown, or cup, they are so termed

Cryptorchid: of male animals: when the testicles have not dropped into the scrotum, but remain in the abdomen: generally infertile

Cull: of deer: selective killing of the surplus, aged, or bad breeding stock

Cup: of antlers: *see Crown*

Deer: generic term for all the cervidae of either sex

Deer forest: in highlands implies an area inhabited by deer, but generally devoid of trees

Deer leap: raised ground outside, or inside, an enclosure allowing deer entrance or egress: commonly used in deer parks to allow wild deer to enter only

Deer park: enclosed area intended to retain a herd of deer

Delayed implantation: of roe doe: delayed growth of the foetus after fertilisation, generally for a period of 4½ months

Dental pad: of deer: the hard pad in front of the upper jaw against which the lower front teeth bite

Dew claws: of hounds and deer: vestigial toes inside leg above pad on hounds, and above cleaves on back of leg in deer

Dished face: of hound, horse, or deer (colloq.): a concave-shaped frontal appearance of the face

Dislodge: of roe deer: to rouse from bed

Doe: the female of roe, fallow, muntjac and Chinese water-deer

Double brows: of antlers: with brow and bay tines

Double head: of a buck: when carrying previous year's antlers along with current year:

Drive: of deer: using beaters to drive deer in front of guns

Droppings: of deer: the faeces: *see Crotties*

Entire: of male animals: with both testicles in the scrotum and functioning

Entry: of deer: gap in edge of wood made by deer

Fag: of red deer: small stag accompanying an old beast

Fat buck: of fallow deer: a buck in prime condition

Fawn: of Chinese water deer, muntjac and fallow deer: the young of either sex in the first year

Feed: of deer: when eating grass or corn: *see Browse*

Fewmets: of deer: old term for droppings, still sometimes used

Final crop: of a plantation of trees: those selected to mature

Flehmen: of deer, horses and most ruminants: behaviour reflex of males, often after savouring female urine, or strange taste: the head is raised and the upper lip curls back while the lower lip droops

Followers: of deer: young beasts following a mature female

Fork: of antlers: the two points on the top of the antler forming a fork

Fray: of a deer: to rub the antlers against a tree, post, or stone

Fraying post, or stock: any post, tree, or stone against which a deer rubs the velvet off its antlers, or later during rut

Gait: of deer: the paces when moving

Gallery: of deer: the tracks, or paths, worn by deer in thick cover

Garron: heavily-built highland pony: trained to carry in the deer carcase in many deer forests

Gaze, at: of deer: when a deer stops feeding to look around, or when it is startled and stops its flight to look back: *see Stand at gaze*

Gillie: often incorrectly spelled ghillie: generally an assistant to the stalker

Glass: of stalking: the term usually applied to a telescope on the hill: hence, to glass the hill, or glassing the hill, when spying the ground

Going back: of a deer's antlers: when they have begun to deteriorate through old age or disease

Gorget: of roe: a white throat patch

Gralloch: of deer: to remove the entrails, stomach, heart and lungs

Grass: of deerstalking: to kill a deer

Groan: of fallow buck: belching sound made when rutting

Ground flora: of a woodland: the lower layer of plant growth

Growth rings: of a deer: the concentric rings often seen in sections of pedicles and in the teeth

Harbour: of a stag: to take up a resting place in a covert

Harbourer: member of the hunt staff whose task it is to advise as to the whereabouts of a suitable deer for hunting

Harem: (colloq.) the following of hinds, or does, acquired by a stag or fallow buck during the rutting season

Havier: of fallow buck: one that has been castrated

Head: of deer: the head and antlers: may refer to antlers alone: hence, a fine head

Headland or headrig: the unploughed edge of a cultivated field: or the strip nearest the hedgerow

Hectare: of land: 2.47 acres

Herbivorous: of animals which eat plants, inc. deer

Herd: of deer: a group: originally of roe, six: fallow or red, twenty

Hide: of deer: the skin

Hide: a place of concealment generally at ground level from which to observe, or shoot, quarry

High seat: a raised platform from which to observe, or shoot, deer: *see Hochsitz*

Hill: stalkers in a deer forest may be said to be on the hill

Hoch-sitz: German term for high seat: also hochstand

Hog-dressed: of a deer: the weight of the carcase minus head, feet and entrails but unskinned

Home range: the area where a deer spends most of its time

Hoop-headed: of a stag: with horns curving upwards but tending to come together

Horns: often incorrectly used to describe antlers

Hummel: of red deer: a male which grows no antlers

Hunt: in Britain the act of following hounds: in most other countries covers also stalking, or any form of game shooting

Imperial: of red deer: term sometimes used without justification to refer to a stag with fourteen points
Inside span: of antlers: the widest measurement between main beams
Interdigital gland: of deer: the scent gland above the cleaves
Intergrade: of deer: a hybrid of two species: e.g. wapiti and red deer
In velvet: of male deer: when antlers are growing and still covered with soft outer skin

John McNab, a: to bag a stag, a grouse and a salmon in one day: so-called after John Buchan's book with that title
Jumps: of deer: places where deer jump over obstacles rather than under, as is normal preference

Kid: of roe deer: the young in first year
Knobber: of red deer: male in second year: also spelled knobbler

Lair: of deer: sometimes used to denote impression left behind where beast has been lying
Length: of antler: measured on the outside edge from the base of the coronet to the tip of the longest top tine
Lodge: of fallow deer: to lie down in lair

Male deer: of red deer: a yearling stag which has not yet grown antlers
March: of highland deer forest: the boundary between estates
Master buck: of fallow deer: buck holding a rutting territory
Melanistic: of deer's colouring: dark hair where lighter hair to be expected
Menil: of fallow deer: a colour variant spotted throughout the year
Metacarpal: of deer or horse: cannon bone of fore leg
Metatarsal: of deer or horse: cannon bone of hind leg
Mewing: of fallow deer: submissive sound made by deer and by fawns: latter also termed peeping
Mixed: of woodland: forest containing both softwood and hardwood trees, i.e. coniferous and deciduous
Monorchid: of animals: male with only one testicle dropped: but usually fertile
Moving: of deer: persuading them to move slowly in a desired direction by letting them scent one's wind, rather than driving them
Murderer: (colloq.) of a deer with switch antlers which can be lethal to other deer

Near: of deer and horse: left hand side: hence near-antler/foreleg
Non-typical: of antlers/colouring: not conforming to the normal pattern
Nott: west country term: hummel

Oestrus: of female animal, inc. deer: the period when 'on heat' or 'in season', i.e. receptive to the male
Off: of deer and horse: the right side: hence: off-antler/fore-leg
Ossification: of antlers: conversion to bone

Outside curve: of antlers: the measurement of an antler from the base to the tip on the outside of the curve

Pace: of deer: speed of movement as measured by the track

Paint: (colloq.) used in New Forest and North America for blood trail left by badly shot deer

Pair: of animals: of same breed but different sex

Palm: of fallow buck: the flat tops of the antlers: such antlers are technically termed palmated, e.g. of reindeer, etc.

Parcel: of hinds: (colloq.) a group

Park: an enclosed area: *see Deer park*

Pass: of deer: the place deer normally cross a hill, river or an obstacle

Pattern: of deer tracks: depends on the pace

Pearling: of antlers: the rough formation on the beam and burr: sometimes termed pearls

Peck-order: of animals: the social gradation of different ages within a group

Pedal-gland: *see Interdigital gland*

Pedicle: of antlers: the bone of the skull from which antlers grow

Peeping: or sometimes pheeping: of fawn: *see Mewing*

Pelage: of animals: the hair

Perruque: of antlers: malformation due to damage to testicles: causing growth of mass resembling wig of this name, sometimes retaining velvet: *see Wig antler*

Piece: (colloq. Scots:) term for sandwiches taken out on hill

Piner: of deer: one that is in poor condition

Pins: of deer: hairs left behind showing that a bullet has hit

Plantation: of trees: an area all planted at the same time

Points: of antlers: alternative for tines

Pre-orbital gland: of deer: scent gland situated near the corner of the eye: *see Sub-orbital gland*

Pricket: of fallow deer: male in second year: but in New Forest used to describe yearling with first spike antlers: also (obs.) red deer in third year

Pronking: of fallow deer: their gait when bouncing away stiff-legged

Quarry: of hunt, or stalker: animal hunted or stalked: derived from the word Quyrreye, or entrails, originally fed to hounds after a hunt

Rack: in plantation: a path cut for purposes of access: in a hedge, a way through

Rack: of deer: (colloq. N. American) antlers

Racks: of deer: paths worn in woodland

Ride: of forest: a broad track separating woodland into blocks

Rifle, the: when stalking: refers to whoever is shooting the deer

Rig: of animal (colloq.): cryptorchid

Rights, to have its': of antlers: when with brows, bays and trays

Roar: of red stag: the sound made during the rut

Roe ring: of roebuck: the circles, or rings, sometimes figures of eight, made by the roebuck chasing the doe during the rut

Rogue: of a deer: when causing serious damage to forestry or crops

Roller: of deer: when falling from a height, as when shot on a steep hillside, thus spoiling the venison

Rouse: of fallow deer: to disturb with hounds when lodged

Royal: of a stag's head having twelve points, with all its rights and three points on top in the form of a cup

Rubbing: of deer: damage caused to trees by deer rubbing antlers

Rubbish: of deer (colloq.): poor animals which should be culled

Rubs: of deer: places where they have rubbed velvet off their antlers

Ruminant: of animals: one which chews the cud: e.g. cattle, deer

Run: of a stag: when condition has been lost as a result of the rut

Rut: of deer: the mating season

Saddle the stag: to load it on the deer saddle of a garron, after gralloching, to take it off the hill

Saddled-up: of garron: when a deer is loaded on the special saddle to take it off the hill

Sanctuary: the part of the forest generally left undisturbed to act as holding ground

Scent: of animals: the smell produced by traces of body oils from the feet

Scent-glands: areas of skin producing strong smelling body oils

Scoring: of deer: the marks left by antlers on the bark of growing trees

Scrape: of deer: marks left by a deer's feet on a patch of ground, probably as a means of marking territory: frequently seen during rut

Season, in: of female animals: the period of the oestrus, or heat

Shed: of antlers: to cast

Shootable beast: of a deer: suitable by virtue of age and condition for shooting

Signs: of deer: by which species, size, age, and sex may be judged

Single: of red deer: the tail

Slot: of deer; the track, or the foot itself

Snag: of antlers: small point

Soar: (obs.) of fallow deer: in fourth year

Soil: of deer: when using a muddy wallow

Span: of antlers: widest distance inside the beams: as opposed to spread

Speculum: of a deer: the part of the rump around the tail

Spellers: of the antlers of a fallow buck: the points, or tines, along the edge of the palm

Spike-buck: of roe-buck having no tines or branches on antlers

Splay: of deer: the spread of the cleaves

Spoor: (colloq.) to track animals: also used of the tracks themselves

Spread: of antlers: the maximum over-all measurement

Spy: with telescope, binoculars or naked eye: to look over ground for deer

Squire: of deer: young stag with older beast: *see also Fag*

Stag: of red or sika deer: the male: not properly so in red deer until fifth year: *see Staggie*: also used to refer to deer of either sex when carted deer are hunted

Staggers: of deer: a disease, resembling sway-back in sheep, causing loss of co-ordination in the hindquarters

Staggie: (colloq.) used in highlands to refer to three- or four-year-old stag: *see Stag*

Stalk: of deer: to approach quietly to get within shot: may be over open or broken ground

Stalker: of deer forest: the professional in charge of the ground

Stand: of fallow buck: the rutting territory

Stand: of rifle: position taken to await deer feeding

Stand at gaze: of deer: to stand watchfully: *see Gaze, at*

Step: of deer track: the distance between one slot and another: from which, along with the depth of imprint, may be gauged the size, age and sex

Stern: of hound: the tail

Still-hunting: of deer: moving extremely slowly through woodland with a rifle, searching for deer: sometimes, incorrectly, used to refer to waiting at a stand when stillness is obligatory for success

Stride: of deer: the space between the impressions of each slot

Stripping: of trees: the removal of bark by teeth of deer

Sub-orbital gland: of deer: the scent gland situated by the inner corner of the eye

Suture line: of the skull of a deer: the demarcation line between adjacent bones

Sway: of tracks: the amount of deviation from a central line: particularly seen in wounded deer

Switch or Switch head: of antlers: having beam and brow points only, or just two beam points

Tallow: of deer; the fat of red, or fallow

Target: (colloq.) of roe deer in winter: the white rump patch

Tatters, in: of velvet: when pieces are hanging from the antlers

Territory: of deer: an area marked by scent glands of male deer on various trees, bushes, stones, etc., to be defended during rut

Thicket: of forestry: the stage of growth between closing of the canopy and the first thinning: implies dense growth of trees and bushes

Thinnings: of forestry: selective cutting and removal of inferior timber from a plantation usually required at three- to six-year intervals

Thrashing: of a fallow buck: as when it flays small trees or bushes with its antlers

Tine: of antlers: each branch, or point

Track: of deer: the footprints, or slot

Trail: of deer: the slots and marks on undergrowth of its passage

Traveller: of deer: one which, for one reason or another, moves over a march, or marches, and does not stay in one deer forest

Tray: of antlers: the third point, or tine
Trophy: of male deer: the head, or antlers
Tush: of red deer: canine tooth in upper jaw: not normally present in fallow
or roe deer
Tush, anal: of roe doe: a white tuft of hair at the lower edge of the target, or
white rump patch of its winter coat

Underplanting: of forestry: introducing a new crop under the partial canopy
of an older plantation
Uneven head: of antlers: when the number of points is uneven it may be
referred to by adding one with prefix uneven: hence, an eleven-pointer
would be an uneven twelve-pointer, etc.

Velvet: of antlers: skin covering them during growth
Venison: of deer; the meat

Wallow: of deer: to take a mud bath: or the hag, or bog, where deer take
mud baths
Wanderer: of a stag: usually with notable head or features, which is known
to frequent two or more forests
Waster: of a deer: a sick or emaciated beast
Well-opened: of antlers: denoting a wide spread
Whickering: (colloq.) of fallow does: sound made during the rut
Whistling: of sika deer: sound made by both sexes: very like a human
whistle
White stag: one that has not been rutting and is not run: *see Run*
Wig antler: of antlers: another name for the malformation termed perruque:
see Perruque
Wind: when stalking: is right, when from deer to stalker: is wrong, when
from stalker towards deer: is cheek wind, when from either right or left:
is flukey, when seemingly changing direction, or fitful

Yearling: of deer: of either sex in its second year
Yeld: of hinds: one which has not had a calf the previous summer, but is not
necessarily barren: *see Blue hind*

Zern, a: a measure of malt whisky: a sufficient quantity taken after stalking,
fishing, or hunting to repel any chill and induce reflective discussion of
the day: hence, a Zernful

Critical Bibliography

Aflalo, F. G., Joint Editor with the Earl of Suffolk and Hedley Peek, *The Encyclopedia of Sport*. Lawrence & Bullen, 1897.
> Aardvark to Zebra: contributions on deer-stalking by A. Grimble, red deer by J. E. Harting, roe deer by J. G. Millais.

Akroyd, Charles H., *A Veteran Sportsman's Diary*. Carruthers, 1926.
> Written, aged 78, after a lifetime of sport: recreates a century of shooting, stalking and fishing at its best.

Aldin, Cecil, *Exmoor*. Witherby, 1935.
> Good on the countryside, deer and hunting with excellent author/artist illustrations.

'An Old Stalker', *Days on the Hill*. Int; Eric Parker. Nisbet, 1926.
> Very revealing reminiscences: particularly good on the character of employers and sportsmen on the hill: human nature unchanging.

Atkinson, G. G., *Red Stags Calling*. A. H. & A. W. Reed, Wellington, 1974.
> Reminiscences of stalking in N.Z., mostly in the Southern Mountains: the sort of material that makes people want to try it for themselves.

Bailey, Dr A. B., *The Functional Deer Stalking Rifle*. Bailey, 1983.
> A very sound nine-page booklet on the stalking rifle obtainable through the British Deer Society.

Baillie, Major the Hon. P. C., J.P., contributor on Red Deer, etc., *Shooting & Stalking* 1983. See Coles, Charles (Editor).

Bertram, James Glass, see 'Ellangowan'.

Blackmore, Howard L., *Hunting Weapons*. Barrie & Jenkins, 1971.
> Covers everything from swords and knives to bows, guns and miscellaneous: worth reading from hunting and historical angles.

Bower, Cdr. J. G., R.N., see 'Klaxon'.

Brander, Michael, *The Hunting Instinct*. Oliver & Boyd, 1964.
> Sub-titled: The Development of Field Sports over the Ages, includes notes on literature, from Twici to 20th century.

Brander, Michael, *Hunting & Shooting*. Weidenfeld & Nicolson, 1971.
> Sub-titled: From the earliest times to the present day, includes deer hunting and stalking in U.K., Europe and around the world.

Brander, Michael, *A Dictionary of Sporting Terms*. A & C Black, 1968.
> Covering all field sports, from angling to hunting: including deer-stalking, and stag-hunting.

Brander, Michael, with Ed. Zern, Joint Editors, *An International Encyclopedia of Shooting*. Rainbird/Pelham, 1972. Peerage Books, 1982.
> An international directory of shooting: includes details of deer stalking around the world: very well illustrated.

Breadalbane, Marchioness of, *High Tops of Black Mount*. Blackwood, 1907.
> Good gripping accounts of deerstalking in late Victorian era: period photographs of authoress in action in long tweed skirt.

Bromley-Davenport, William, *Sport*. Maclehose, 1933.
> Two chapters on stalking, one on reindeer in Norway and one on red deer in the Highlands: irritatingly egotistical and dated style.

Browning, T. O., B.Sc., Ph.D, *Animal Populations*. Hutchinson, 1963.
> An introduction to the scientific study of animal populations: covers effects of environment, weather, interaction of varied factors.

Budgett, H. M., *Hunting by Scent*. Eyre and Spottiswoode, 1933.
> Fascinating discourse by ex-M.H. on origins and dissemination of scent in varying conditions: with pictures by Lionel Edwards.

Burrard, Major Sir Gerald, *Notes on Sporting Rifles*. Arnold, 1920.
> 1953 reprint mirrors the considerable changes that have taken place in sporting rifles: e.g. comments on d.bs and telescopic sights.

Cadman, Arthur, *Dawn, Dusk & Deer*. Country Life, 1966.
> A recognised authority on deer as well as a gifted writer conveying his enthusiasm for his quarry: well illustrated by C. F. Tunnicliffe.

Cameron, Allan Gordon, *The Wild Red Deer of Scotland*. Blackwood, 1923.
> Interesting late Edwardian viewpoint on stalking in the Highlands and islands: four chapters on antlers, four on land reform.

Cameron, of Lochiel, *Red Deer*. Fur & Feather Series, Longmans, 1896.
> Contributor of section entitled Deer Stalking, interesting on management of deer forest and the practice of deer-stalking, very practical.

Carhart, Arthur C., *Hunting North American Deer*. Macmillan, N.Y., 1946.
> Covers mule deer and white-tail: good points on preparations for stalking and on dealing with a newly-shot deer.

Chalmers, Patrick R., *Mine Eyes to the Hills*. A & C Black, 1931.
> Sub-titled: An Anthology of the Highland Forest, well illustrated by V. R. Balfour-Browne, very evocative and wide-ranging.

Chalmers, Patrick R., *Deerstalking*. Sportsmans Library, Philip Allan, 1936.
> Very sound account of deerstalking as conducted in the mid-1930s, now somewhat dated, especially regarding the prices quoted.

Chalmers, Patrick R., *Field Sports of Scotland*. Philip Allan, 1936.
> A delightful very readable chapter on roe deer: very sound on the establishment of an ideal 'Roe Forest' and on stalking.

Chaplin, R. E., *Deer*. Blandford Press, 1977.
> Covers world deer scientifically and concisely with much of interest on deer in Britain. Well illustrated.

Chapman, Abel, *Retrospect*. Gurney & Jackson, 1928.
> Sub-titled: Reminiscences of a hunter-naturalist, 1851–1928, one good chapter on shooting in highlands, well worth reading.

Chapman, Donald and Norma, *Fallow Deer*. Terence Dalton, 1975.
> Sub-titled: Their history, distribution and biology, a scientific study in depth with excellent photographs by J. K. Fawcett.

Christy, Theodore, *Random Recollections*. Bentham, no date.
> Very disjointed sporting reminiscences including four years as Master of Essex Staghounds pre-1914.

Cockburn, Lt. Col., R.H.A., Contributor on Deer Management, *Shooting and Stalking*, 1983: see Coles, Charles (Editor) below.

Coles, Charles (Editor), *Shooting and Stalking*. Stanley Paul, 1983.
Includes 64 condensed pages on stalking deer: contributions by P. C. Baillie, R. H. A. Cockburn, R. Prior, R. W. Rayson, C. G. Wright.

Collyns, Dr Charles Palk, *The Chase of the Wild Red Deer*. Longmans, 1862.
The first history of staghunting in Devon and Somerset, from Queen Elizabeth I, with records from 1780, good material.

Colquhoun, John, *Sporting Days*. Blackwood, 1866.
Wide-ranging Victorian sporting recollections: one chapter on deer driving in Mull and another on roe shooting in Aberdeenshire.

Colquhoun, John, *The Moor & The Loch*. 5th 2 Vol edn. Blackwood, 1880.
Two vols of highland sporting reminiscences: only one chapter on red deer stalking, one on roe, good of period.

Conway, James, *Forays among Salmon and Deer*. T. D. Morison. No date.
Good early material on deer stalking around 1860s, with some poaching stories. Illustrates difficulties of muzzle loaders.

Corballis, James Henry, Ed. A. J. Fisher, *Forty-Five Years of Sport*. Bentley, 1891.
Some very revealing material on the developments in Scottish deer forests during the late Victorian period: good on stalking.

Crealock, Lt. Gen. Henry H., C.B., C.M.G., *Deer Stalking in the Highlands of Scotland*, ed. by Maj Gen. J. N. Crealock, C.B., 250 copies, Longmans, 1892.
Highly evocative accounts of 22 years stalking red deer in highlands: illustrated by drawings of gifted author, good tips to be gleaned.

Dalrymple, Byron W., *The Complete Book of Deer Hunting*. Stoeger, 1973.
Very good on deer stalking in general, even if naturally orientated towards the U.S.A., but some useful points for stalkers in the U.K.

Daniel, Rev. William B., *Rural Sports*. Longmans, 1801.
Three volumes and a supplement on sports of the day, but entries relating to deer are minimal: no mention of stalking.

Darling, F. Fraser, *A Herd of Red Deer*. Oxford, 1937.
A scientific study of a red deer herd in Wester Ross: has some very useful points to make relative to stalking, deer behaviour and sheep.

Day, J. Wentworth, *The Dog in Sport*. Harrap, 1938.
Some fairly superficial material on deerhounds with quotations from Scrope and other sources.

Day, James Wentworth, *They Walk the Wild Places*. Blandford, 1956.
Three chapters on deer, fairly florid prose, but readable, mentions all deer in Britain and hog deer for good measure.

de Nahlik, A. J., *Wild Deer*. Faber & Faber, 1951.
Some very good material on roe, fallow and red deer: from trophies to spoor, from high seats to ballistics, from tracking to cooking.

Dobie, W. G. M., *Game-Bag and Creel*. W. Green, 1927.

A collection of unusual sporting verse, several on deer stalking: attractively illustrated in colour by V. Balfour-Browne.

Duff, K. R., see Harris, Roy A., co-author of *Wild Deer in Britain*.

Dryden, Alice, *The Art of Hunting*. Mark, 1908.
Annotated reprint of Twici's *Art of Hunting*, also *La Chasse du Cerf* and *Craft of Venery*.

Dryden, Sir Henry, *The Art of Hunting*. London, 1844.
First annotated reprint of William Twici's *Art of Hunting*: first scholarly criticism.

Ebrington, Viscount, *Red Deer*. Fur & Feather Series, Longmans, 1896.
Contributor of section entitled: Stag-hunting. Competent condensed account of stag-hunting in France and Britain. Well worth reading.

Edwards, Lionel, and Wallace, Harold Frank, *The Pursuit of Red, Fallow and Roe Deer in England and Scotland*. Longmans, 1927.
Superbly illustrated in the grand manner with good material on deer in the Highlands and Lowlands of Scotland and England.

'Ellangowan' (J. G. Bertram), *Outdoor Sports of Scotland*. W. H. Allen, 1890.
Wide-ranging, with only three chapters on deer stalking, but very good on the background of the sports.

Elwes, H. J., F.R.S., *Memoirs*. Benn, 1930.
Sporting autobiography, mostly abroad, but including a chapter on the deer forests of Scotland.

Fisher, A. J., Ed., *Forty-Five Years of Sport*. 1891. See Corballis, James Henry.

Fittis, Robert Scott, *Sports & Pastimes of Scotland*. Gardner, 1891.
Includes a very cursory and superficial description of the development of the Scottish deer forests.

Forbes, J., Ed., Wilson, R. A., *New Zealand Deer Heads*. Country Life, 1924.
Pictures of all the record red deer and wapiti heads exhibited at the British Empire Exhibition: with an introduction and maps.

Forrester, Rex and Illingworth, Neil., *Hunting in New Zealand*. Reed, 1966.
Some very good pointers on shooting, of use not only in New Zealand: covers red deer, fallow, sika, chamois, thar, wild goat and pig.

Fortescue, Hon. John., *Stag-hunting on Exmoor*. Chapman and Hall, 1887.
Records of the hunt from 1855 to 1881 added on to Dr C. P. Collyn's history: some interesting material.

Fortescue, Hon. J. W., *The Story of a Red Deer*. Macmillan, 1925.
Accurate account of life of Exmoor stag, with powers of speech: good illustrations by G. D. Armour.

Fraser, Sir Hugh, *Amid the High Hills*. A & C Black, 1934.
Reminiscences of an experienced sportsman, including salmon fishing and grouse shooting: some good stalking anecdotes.

Gathorne-Hardy, A. E., *Autumns in Argyleshire*. Longmans, 1900.
Good period sporting anecdotes, including the stalking of fallow, roe and red deer: excellent illustrations by Thorburn.

Gathorne-Hardy, A. E., *My Happy Hunting Grounds*. Longmans, 1914.

Some good late Edwardian sporting reminiscences: not a lot on stalking, but good period anecdotes.

Gibson, Colin, *Highland Deer Stalker*. Seeley Service, 1958.
A biography of stalker Allan Cameron of Glenmuik in south-east Grampians 1882–1950s: good portrait of changes in life in the hills.

Gilbert, John M., *Hunting Reserves in Mediaeval Scotland*. Donald, 1979.
Scholarly research covering some interesting aspects of Scottish deer hunting and the laws from eleventh to sixteenth centuries.

Gordon, Seton, *Hebridean Memories*. Cassell, 1923.
Not a great deal on deer, but like all Seton Gordon's books, well observed, well written and well worth reading.

Gordon, Seton, *The Cairngorm Hills of Scotland*. Cassell, 1925.
Not much on deer, but some very interesting naturalist's notes on the Cairngorms before ski-ing.

Gordon, Seton, *A Highland Year*. Eyre & Spottiswode, 1944.
A naturalist's record of the changing year in the Highlands: not much on deer, but some very interesting nature observations.

Goss, Fred, Ed., Dr H. Campbell Thomson, *Memories of a Stag Harbourer*. Witherby, 1931.
Very good reading and excellent comments on deer on Exmoor, particularly good on tracking.

Grimble, A., contributor on deer-stalking to *The Encyclopedia of Sport*. 1987, see Aflolo, F. G., Joint Editor.

Grimble, Augustus, *Highland Sport*. Chapman & Hall, 1894.
Authentic and amusing Victorian accounts of sport in the Highlands, reminiscent of Surtees: beautifully illustrated by Thorburn.

Grimble, A., *Deer Stalking*. Chapman & Hall, 550 copies only, 1888.
Still has some very sound advice to give on stalking on the hill, on deer and their behaviour; good reading as well.

Grimble, A., *The Deer Forests of Scotland*. Kegan Paul. 500 copies only, 1896.
Covers in detail most of the Scottish deer forests with anecdotes: some details on deer shot. Good reading.

Grimble, A., *Deer-Stalking and Deer Forests of Scotland*. Kegan Paul, 1901.
Combines above books on deer stalking (1888) and on the deer forests (1896): each complementary to other: good interesting material.

Hare, C.E., *The Language of Sport*. Country Life, 1939.
A dictionary of terms relating to sport: includes many ancient hunting terms relating to deer.

Harms, Lt. Col. Roy C., *Young or Old?* Verlag Mayer, 1966.
Translated from Herbert Krebs' original German text: 70 pictures of roe with comments on age, antlers, etc., see Krebs, Herbert.

Harris, Roy A., with Duff, K. R., *Wild Deer in Britain*. David & Charles, 1970.
Excellent illustrations and good text by author/photographers on natural history of all species of deer found in Britain.

Hart-Davis, Duff, *Monarchs of the Glen*. Cape, 1978.
  A history of red deer stalking in the Highlands, starting with the geological formations and progressing to the present day.
Hart-Davis, Capt. H., *Stalking Sketches*. Horace Cox, 1904.
  With seventeen good illustrations by the author: a pleasantly dated Edwardian book on stalking in the highlands.
Harting, J. E., contributor on red deer to *The Encyclopedia of Sport*. 1897. See Aflalo, F. G., Joint Editor.
Hartley, Gilfrid W., *Wild Sport, With Gun, Rifle and Salmon-Rod*. William Blackwood, 1903.
  Some excellent well-written material on deer stalking with some still sound advice on shooting.
Hartley, Gilfrid W., *Wild Sport and Some Stories*. William Blackwood, 1912.
  Some very good illustrations, black and white and colour, but not as much on deer as his first book.
Hayes, Tom, *Hunting the White-tail Deer*. A. S. Barnes, N.Y., 1960.
  Interesting on calibres and very good on still-hunting, some frightening anecdotes on shooting in N. America.
Hewett, H. F., *The Fairest Hunting*. J. A. Allen, 1963.
  Includes a summary of the stag-hunting seasons on Exmoor from 1936–60, with notes on the deer, deer fences, hounds and harbourer.
Holden, Philip, *The Deer Hunters*. Hodder & Stoughton, 1976.
  Journalistic articles on deer stalking in New Zealand: gives an unattractive picture of the shooting and shooting conditions.
Holmes, Dr Frank, *Following the Roe*. Bartholomew, 1973.
  Good scientific observer/stalker material on background natural history of the roe by a life-time enthusiast: very well illustrated.
Ivrea, Marquis, see 'Snaffle'.
Kennedy, Captain Henry Shaw, contributor on deer stalking to *The Keeper's Book*. See Mackie, Sir Peter Jeffrey, Bart.
'Klaxon' (Cdr. J. G. Bower, R.N.), *Heather Mixture*. Blackwood, 1922.
  Good rousing sporting novel with almost everything including good stalk of fallow buck.
Krebs, Herbert, author of *Young or Old?* See Harms, Lt. Col. Roy C.
Latymer, Lord, *Stalking in Scotland & New Zealand*. Blackwood, 1935.
  Writing and recollections somewhat dated: mainly on trophy hunting: interesting to contrast conditions then and now in both countries.
Leggatt, Dr Ashley, *Stalking Reminiscences: 1914–1920*. John Murray, 1921.
  One hundred and fourteen pages as the title indicates of leaves from the Game Book of a novice stalker near Beauly.
Leggatt, Ashley, *Still Stalking & Talking*. John Murray, 1926.
  Eighty-eight pages from the author's stalking diaries in various parts of the highlands from 1921 to 1925 inclusive.
Leopold, Aldo, *Game Management*, Scribner's, 1933.

An extremely competent and thorough investigation of all aspects of game management, including deer, in the U.S.A.

McDiarmid, Dr A., M.R.C.V.S: see Prior, Richard, *The Roe Deer of Cranborne Chase*: contributor of chapters on diseases and parasites.

McDiarmid, Dr A., M.R.C.V.S., *Roe Deer*, Game Conservancy, 1978.
Contributor to Roe Deer Management and Stalking booklet: on causes of mortality and disease.

Mackenzie, Evan G., *Grouse Shooting & Deer Stalking*. Love, 1907.
Some quite interesting comments on the state of stalking at this period and some good descriptions of the Edwardian scene.

Mackenzie, Osgood Hanbury, *A Hundred Years in the Highlands*. Arnold, 1921, Bles, 1949.
Family reminiscences covering a hundred years of life in the Highlands: good material including some on early deer-stalking.

Mackie, Sir Peter Jeffrey, Bart., *The Keeper's Book*. Foulis, 1904.
Some points in the chapter on deer by Captain Henry Shaw Kennedy, but a splendid period piece of a book that went to 15 reprints.

MacNally, Lea, *Highland Deer Forest*. Dent, 1970.
Good naturalist recollections of the hill by ex-stalker turned Nature Warden: first rate photographs and very readable style.

Lea, *The Year of the Red Deer*. Dent, 1975.
100 black and white photographs and 8 pages in colour with supporting text: both of a high standard by the author.

Macpherson, The Rev. H. A., *Red Deer*. Fur & Feather Series, Longmans, 1896.
Contributor of section entitled Natural History: not a great deal of interest to be found.

Macrae, Alexander, *A Handbook of Deer-Stalking*. Blackwood, 1880.
Somewhat dated and slightly stilted, but good basic material by an expert stalker of the period, with much still applicable.

Maxwell, Sir Herbert, *Memoirs of the Months*. Maclehose, 1897/1931.
Sub-titled. Pages from the notebook of a field-naturalist and antiquary: very little on deer, but some interesting nature notes.

McConnachie, A. I., *The Deer & Deer Forests of Scotland*. Witherby, 1923.
Provides a list of deer forests and owners with some interesting anecdotal reminiscences, also a background history and development.

McConnachie, A. I., *Deer Stalking in Scotland*. Witherby, 1924.
Stalking anecdotes quoted from many sources varying from stalkers to landowners: some interesting material of the Edwardian period.

McConnachie, Alexander Inkson, *Deer Forest Life*. Maclehose, 1932.
Reminiscences and anecdotes of stalkers on the hill: a good deal of interest to the naturalist as well as the deer stalker.

Millais, J. G., F.Z.S., contributor on roe deer to *The Encyclopedia of Sport*, 1897. See Aflalo, F. G., Joint Editor.

Millais, John G., F.Z.S., *British Deer and Their Horns*. Sotheran, 1897.

Some excellent illustrations, b/w and colour, by author, Landseer and others: includes sections on roe and fallow as well as red deer.

Millais, J. G., F.Z.S., *Wanderings and Memories*. Longmans, 1919.
Autobiography including one very good chapter on deerstalking in 1918 of the leaves from my gamebook variety.

Milling, J. Chapman, *Buckshot & Hounds*. A. S. Barnes, N.Y., 1867.
Advice on deer driving to shotguns in S. Carolina: shotguns preferred to rifles on safety grounds in U.S. Good on dealing with carcase.

Mowbraye, John., Ed., *Baxter's Game Book*. Hamish Hamilton, 1973.
Collection of verse and prose with a certain amount on deer hunting and stalking, some much used, but some less well known.

O'Connor, Jack, *The Hunting Rifle*. Stoeger Publishing Co. 1970.
Naturally has a fairly strong transatlantic flavour in choice of rifles, but very good on telescopic sights and shooting.

Ogilvie, Will H., *Over the Grass*. Constable, 1925.
Sporting verse, mainly on hunting, illustrated by Lionel Edwards: only two pictures of deer, but both are excellent.

Orr, Willie, *Deer Forests, Landlords & Crofters*. Donald, 1982.
Mainly research on the ownership of the highland deer forests, intended more as a political thesis than a book on deer.

Parker, Eric, *Field, River and Hill*. Philip Allan, 1927.
Hotchpotch of reprinted sporting articles from *The Field* and other publications: some on deer in the hills, disappointing on the whole.

Parker, Eric, *English Wild Life*. Longmans, 1929
Somewhat illogically has a section on highland deer stalking, also mention of roe and fallow: not a great deal of interest.

Peek, Hedley, Joint Editor with F. G. Aflalo and the Earl of Suffolk, *The Encyclopedia of Sport*. Lawrence & Bullen, 1897. See Aflalo F. G.

Perry, Richard, *In the High Grampians*. Lindsay Drummond, 1948.
A naturalist's record of two years spent in the Grampians area: hardly anything on deer, but some evocative material on the hills.

Perry, Richard, *The Watcher and the Deer*. David & Charles, 1971.
Naturalist study of red deer in the Grampians and Cairngorms written in the third person which makes tiresome reading at times.

Portland, the Duke of, *Fifty Years of Sport*. Faber & Faber, 1933.
Disjointed but interesting account of varied sport over fifty years in Caithness with some good stalking anecdotes.

Prichard, H. Hesketh, *Sport in Wildest Britain*. Philip Allan, 1930.
Nothing on deer, but an excellent writer on sport including stalking of wildfowl, capercailzie and seals.

Prior, Richard, contributor on *Roe Deer, Shooting & Stalking*. 1983, see Coles, Charles (Editor).

Prior, Richard, *Roe Stalking*. S. T. Library, 1963.
A good simple introduction to the subject: a how-to book covering all that a beginner requires to know: now a little dated.

Prior, Richard, *Living with Deer*. André Deutsch, 1965.
An attractively written book, covering red, roe, fallow, sika and muntjac: pleasantly readable: some good illustrations.

Prior, Richard, *The Roe Deer of Cranborne Chase*. O.U.P., 1968.
'An Ecological Study' after four years groundwork, with chapters on diseases and parasites: see Dr A. McDiarmid: excellent photographs.

Prior, Richard, *Roe Deer, Management & Stalking*. Game Conservancy, 1978.
A very good booklet, concisely covering the subject: section on disease by Dr A. McDiarmid.

Rayson, R. W., contributor with C. G. Wright on Firearms for Deer, *Shooting & Stalking*. 1983. See Coles, Charles (Editor).

Sandys-Winsch, Godfrey, B.A., *Gun Law*. 4th Edn., Shaw, 1985.
A useful 150-page compendium of all aspects of the law relating to shotguns and rifles.

Scrope, William, *Days of Deer Stalking*. John Murray, 1839.
Rather tedious reading nowadays, but still noteworthy as the first book to be written solely on deer stalking in the Highlands.

Shand, Alexander Innes, *Red Deer*. Fur & Feather Series, Longmans, 1896.
Contributor to the Cookery of Venison section: wordy and very limited in scope: not worth inclusion.

Smillie, I. S., *A Guide to Stalking Red Deer in Scotland*. Regency, 1983.
Some good instructional material, well set out: as the title indicates unfortunately restricted to the red deer in the Highlands.

Smith, W. McCombie, *The Romance of Poaching*. Mackay, 1904.
Biographies of Alexander Davidson (1782–1843) and John Farquharson (1823–1893) eulogistic accounts of early Highland deer poachers.

'Snaffle' (Marquis Ivrea), *Roe deer*. Privately Printed, 1904.
The first book written entirely on roe deer: mostly on hunting with hounds, but one chapter on the roe in heraldry.

Soper, Eileen A., *Muntjac*. Longmans, 1969.
Observations over eight years in a Hertfordshire garden well illustrated and observed by author/artist.

Speedy, Tom, *Sport in the Highlands & Lowlands*. Blackwood, 1884.
One chapter on deer stalking of limited interest: does, however, emphasise the importance of knowing the ground in the Highlands.

Stapledon, Richard, *Exmoor, Elegance & Rhythm*. Stapledon, 1968.
Ramblings of a prep-school headmaster on edge of Exmoor: some points of interest for the persevering reader.

St John, Charles, *Wild Sports of the Highlands*. John Murray, 1845.
Excellent writer on roe deer and red deer stalking: one of the everreadable classics on deer and deer stalking.

Stuart, J. S & C. E., *Lays of the Deer Forest*. Two vols., Blackwood, 1848.
Volume One: entirely full of appalling verse by brothers John Sobieski and Charles Edward, who dubiously claimed direct Stuart descent.
Volume Two: has some quite readable material on early deer

hunting in the Highlands; but brothers almost as turgid in prose as verse.

Suffolk, Earl of, Joint Editor, with F. G. Aflalo and Hedley Peek, *The Encyclopedia of Sport*. Lawrence & Bullen, 1897. See Aflalo, F. G.

Taylor Page, F. J., *Field Guide to British Deer*. Mammal Society, 1957.
The first field guide for popular use produced by the Secretary of the Mammal Society's Deer Group and others, 3rd Edn., 1982.

Taylor Page, F. J., *Roe Deer*. Animals of Britain Series, *The Sunday Times*, 1963.
Twenty-two page booklet: excellent photographs and good if slightly dated text by the Secretary of the Mammal Society's Deer Group.

Tegner, Henry, *The Roe Deer*. Batchworth, 1951.
An excellent if now slightly dated book on almost all aspects of the roe deer and its pursuit.

Tegner, Henry, *The Buck of Lordenshaw*. Batchworth Press, 1953.
Good fictional account of roe deer's life cycle based on observations of a Northumbrian stalker.

Tegner, Henry, *The Sporting Rifle and its use in Britain*. Jenkins, 1962.
Very authoritative on all aspects of rifle shooting, particularly good on all types of deer stalking.

Tegner, Henry, *Game for the Sporting Rifle*. Jenkins, 1963.
Chapters on red, roe and fallow deer down to squirrels and rats by an author who is always interesting and readable.

Vesey-Fitzgerald, Brian, *British Game*. Collins, 1946.
Three chapters on deer: red, fallow and roe, with excellent illustrations: short but worth reading.

Vesey-Fitzgerald, Brian, *The Domestic Dog*. Routledge & Kegan Paul, 1957.
The dog discussed in history, art, literature and sport: very little on deer or deer hounds.

Wallace, Harold Frank and Edwards, Lionel, *The pursuit of Red, Fallow and Roe Deer in England and Scotland*. Longmans, 1927. See Edwards, Lionel.

Wallace, H. Frank, *A Highland Gathering*. Eyre & Spottiswode, 1932.
Sub-titled: Some Leaves from a Stalker's Diary, indicative of contents: particularly good on roe stalking in the Highlands.

Watson, Alfred E. T., *Red Deer*. Fur & Feather Series, Longmans, 1896.
General Editor: The Fur and Feather Series. See the Rev. H. A. Macpherson, Cameron of Lochiel, Viscount Ebrington, A. I. Shand.

Watson, J. E. P., *Victorian and Edwardian Field Sports*. Batsford, 1978.
Period photographs with minimal text covering most aspects of field sports; small section on deerstalking.

Whitaker, J., F.Z.S., *Deer Parks and Paddocks of England*. Ballantyne, 1892.
Descriptions of around 400 deer parks and paddocks, down to those of 10 acres with wire fences and only 24 deer.

Whitehead, G. K., *Deer & Their Management*. Country Life, 1950.
Comprehensive volume on the management of deer in the deer parks of Great Britain and Ireland.

Whitehead, G. K., *The Deerstalking Grounds of G.B & I.* Hollis & Carter, 1960.
> The most complete record of the deer forests of Scotland and their owners yet, with records of deer killed: the standard work.

Whitehead, G. K., *The Deer of Great Britain & Ireland.* Routledge, 1964.
> Covers the distribution of all existing types of deer in Britain and Ireland, also their historical antecedents.

Whitehead G. K., *Deer Stalking in Scotland.* S.T. Library, 1964.
> A simple how-to introduction: covers the stalk and the shot: dealing with the deer: the equipment required.

Whitehead, G. K., *Deer of the World.* Constable, 1972.
> Well illustrated: covering world deer and including an appendix, maps of distribution and a bibliography.

Whitehead, G. K., *Hunting & Stalking Deer.* Batsford, 1980.
> A historical record of hunting deer in Britain and Ireland: including stalking: a great deal packed into the one book.

Whitehead, G. K., *Stalking Deer Throughout the World.* Batsford, 1982.
> A comprehensive international directory of hunting and stalking deer: including details of trophy measurements.

Williams, John, *An Introduction to Hunting.* J. A. Allen, 1973.
> A sixty-page introductory booklet on hunting for Pony Club members: good on deer hunting in Somerset.

Williamson, Henry, *The Wild Red Deer of Exmoor.* Faber & Faber, 1931.
> Sixty-four pages by the author of *Tarka the Otter* on the logic, ethics and economics of staghunting: on the whole in favour.

Willoughby de Broke, Lord, *The Passing Years.* Constable, 1924.
> Autobiography of keen huntsman M. F. H., also includes an excellent account of deerstalking in the highlands: well worth reading.

Winans, Walter, F. Z. S., *The Sporting Rifle.* Putnam, 1908.
> Interesting material on driven red deer shooting: one chapter on roe shooting: poorly faked photographs do not enhance text.

Winans, Walter, F. Z. S., *Deer Breeding for Fine Heads.* Rowland Ward, 1913.
> Only an Edwardian millionaire could have written some of the advice given: shows him amid seventy fallow does shot in one day.

Wright, C. G., Lt. Col., contributor on Deer Stalking, etc., *Shooting & Stalking.* 1983. See Coles, Charles (Editor).

Zern, Ed. with Michael Brander, Joint Editors, *An International Encyclopedia of Shooting.* Rainbird/Pelham Books, 1972. Peerage Books, 1982. See Brander, Michael.

Zern, Ed., *Hunting & Fishing from A to Zern.* Nick Lyons Books, 1985.
> These chronicles of sporting travel are full of quaint and laughable anecdote but are no substitute for *Arnold's Guide to World Air Routes.*